CONOR McPHERSON

Conor McPherson was born in Dublin in 1971. Plays include *Rum and Vodka* (Fly by Night Theatre Co., Dublin); *The Good Thief* (Dublin Theatre Festival; Stewart Parker Award); *This Lime Tree Bower* (Fly by Night Theatre Co. and Bush Theatre, London; Meyer-Whitworth Award); *St Nicholas* (Bush Theatre and Primary Stages, New York); *The Weir* (Royal Court, London, Duke of York's, West End and Walter Kerr Theatre, New York; Laurence Olivier, Evening Standard, Critics' Circle, George Devine Awards); *Dublin Carol* (Royal Court and Atlantic Theater, New York); *Port Authority* (Ambassadors Theatre, West End, Gate Theatre, Dublin and Atlantic Theater, New York); *Shining City* (Royal Court, Gate Theatre, Dublin and Manhattan Theatre Club, New York; Tony Award nomination for Best Play); *The Seafarer* (National Theatre, London, Abbey Theatre, Dublin and Booth Theater, New York; Laurence Olivier, Evening Standard, Tony Award nominations for Best Play); *The Veil* (National Theatre) and *The Night Alive* (Donmar Warehouse). Theatre adaptations include Daphne du Maurier's *The Birds* (Gate Theatre, Dublin and Guthrie Theater, Minneapolis) and August Strindberg's *The Dance of Death* (Donmar at Trafalgar Studios).

Work for the cinema includes *I Went Down*, *Saltwater*, Samuel Beckett's *Endgame*, *The Actors*, and *The Eclipse*. He also adapted John Banville's *Elegy for April* for the BBC.

Awards for his screenwriting include three Best Screenplay Awards from the Irish Film and Television Academy; Spanish Cinema Writers Circle Best Screenplay Award; the CICAE Award for Best Film Berlin Film festival; Jury Prize San Sebastian Film Festival; and the Méliès d'Argent Award for Best European Film.

Other Titles in this Series

Conor McPherson

THE NIGHT ALIVE

NICK HERN BOOKS

London

www.nickhernbooks.co.uk

A Nick Hern Book

The Night Alive first published in 2013 by Nick Hern Books Limited,
The Glasshouse, 49a Goldhawk Road, London W12 8QP

The Night Alive copyright © 2013 Conor McPherson

Conor McPherson has asserted his moral right to be identified as the author of
this work

Cover image by AKA
Cover design by Ned Hoste, 2H

Typeset by Nick Hern Books, London
Printed and bound in Great Britain by CPI Group (UK) Ltd

A CIP catalogue record for this book is available from the British Library

ISBN   978 1 84842 336 7

The Night Alive was first performed at the Donmar Warehouse,
London, on 19 June 2013 (previews from 13 June), with the
following cast:

AIMEE	Caoilfhionn Dunne
KENNETH	Brian Gleeson
TOMMY	Ciarán Hinds
DOC	Michael McElhatton
MAURICE	Jim Norton

Director	Conor McPherson
Designer	Soutra Gilmour
Lighting Designer	Neil Austin
Sound Designer	Gregory Clarke
Casting Director	Alastair Coomer CDG

'When they saw the star they rejoiced. They went into the house and they saw Mary and her child. And falling to their knees they offered their gifts of gold and frankincense and myrrh.'

Matthew 2:11–12

Characters

MAURICE, *seventies*
TOMMY, *fifties*
AIMEE, *late twenties*
DOC, *forties*
KENNETH, *late thirties*

Dialogue in square brackets [ ] is unspoken.

Setting

An Edwardian house near the Phoenix Park in Dublin.

Autumn. The present.

This text went to press before the end of rehearsals and so may differ slightly from the play as performed.

The first-floor drawing room of an Edwardian house near the Phoenix Park in Dublin. High double doors lead to a small metal balcony with steps down to the rear garden. The room is now a bedsit. It is cluttered and messy. Boxes of knick-knacks and old newspapers and magazines are piled into corners, spilling out on to a single bed on one side of the room and a camp bed on the other. There is a battered old armchair, a foldaway chair or two. A door leads to a little toilet that has been built in one corner. Another door leads to the landing and the rest of the house.

There is a little gas hob and a sink with dirty dishes and saucepans piled into it. There is a framed poster of Steve McQueen on his motorbike from the movie The Great Escape, *a framed poster of Marvin Gaye's album cover,* What's Going On?, *and two posters advertising Finland as a holiday destination.*

As the play begins, moonlight pours in through the double doors from the balcony. The door to the hallway is open and electric light spills in from the landing. An elderly gentleman, MAURICE, *is standing in the room looking out at the garden. He wears pyjamas and a dressing gown and carries a walking stick. He stands still for a moment until distant church bells and a dog barking somewhere stir him from his reverie. He looks about the room in disgust. He lifts a garment or two with his stick, wondering how anyone can live like this. He hears voices approaching and hurries quietly off upstairs.*

We hear voices coming from the garden:

TOMMY (*offstage*). Now, that's it. Yeah. This is it. Up the steps. Are you alright? That's it. Head back. Nice and easy. Around here now. This is us.

We see TOMMY *leading* AIMEE *in. He is in his fifties, well built but well worn. She is in her twenties, skinny and also well worn. She holds her head back, pressing* TOMMY*'s Dublin Gaelic football tracksuit top to her face. It is covered in blood. She stands there while* TOMMY *goes and switches on a little lamp.*

Come in we'll sit you down and we can have a look.

The lamp blinks off again.

Ah balls! Hold on. You don't have a euro? No, it's alright. I'll jimmy the lock. I'll just grab this.

He goes to a few drawers and roots noisily around unsuccessfully in the gloom before he finally finds a hammer amid the detritus on the counter. He takes the hammer and uses it to tap the meter open. He takes a coin from the drawer and sticks it back in the slot.

Out she pops and back in the slot.

He turns the dial and the lamp pops back on again.

Now. That's it.

He climbs down off the chair.

Now come here till we have a look at you. Sit down here. There we go.

He shifts a pile of crap off the armchair and sits AIMEE *down.*

AIMEE. Your jacket is wrecked.

TOMMY. Don't mind that, I'll bang that in the washing machine. Show me.

AIMEE *lets* TOMMY *gently pull the tracksuit top away from her face. Her nose has bled down her chin and onto her clothes.* TOMMY *adjusts her head so he can see.*

Well, the bleeding has stopped.

AIMEE. Is it broken?

TOMMY. I don't know, love – it looks swollen.

AIMEE. I have a big nose anyway.

TOMMY. Like very big?

AIMEE. Big enough.

TOMMY. Was it always crooked?

AIMEE. Yeah, a bit.

TOMMY. Crooked to the left or the right?

AIMEE. The left.

TOMMY. To my left?

AIMEE. Yeah.

TOMMY. Okay. Then I don't think he broke it.

TOMMY goes rooting through a cupboard near the sink. He finds a little plastic bowl and a tea towel.

Do you think you might get sick again?

AIMEE. No.

He runs some water and wets the towel, bringing the bowl to AIMEE.

TOMMY. You can use this if you are.

AIMEE. Thanks.

She holds the bowl on her lap.

TOMMY. Up to me, love, we wipe this up a bit.

She raises her face to him and winces while he wipes her face.

Wup, sorry, too hard. That alright?

AIMEE *gives a tiny nod.* TOMMY *cleans her face. She takes the towel from him and cleans it herself.*

God, I wonder should we ring an ambulance.

AIMEE. No.

TOMMY. No?

AIMEE. No, it'll be alright.

TOMMY. I could run you down to the hospital.

AIMEE. No, they'll ring the guards.

TOMMY. Will they?

AIMEE. Yeah, they'll think it was you.

TOMMY. They'd think it was me?!

AIMEE. Probably.

TOMMY. Well, look… I certainly don't need that, so…

AIMEE. I don't want the guards.

TOMMY. No, you don't want the bleeding guards in all over it. (*Looks at her face.*) Well, now I'm not an expert, but in my [opinion]… I would say, that it's probably going to be [alright]… You see, I've no ice! I've no fridge!

He throws his eye ineffectually around the room for something that might substitute for ice.

AIMEE. Can I use your bathroom?

TOMMY. Yeah! (*Indicating the door in the corner of the room.*) There's a little toilet in there, or there's a bigger, proper bathroom down the landing out there.

AIMEE. No that's fine.

AIMEE gets up.

TOMMY. Wait, hold on.

TOMMY bolts towards the little loo. He switches the light on and goes in. We hear the toilet flush. TOMMY bangs around trying to make it presentable. AIMEE stands waiting, gingerly touching her nose. She goes to a little mirror above the sink and has a look. TOMMY comes out, grabs a two-pack of toilet rolls, smiles apologetically at AIMEE, holding them up, and disappears inside the loo again, and emerges, wiping his hands.

There you go.

AIMEE. Thanks.

TOMMY. Do you want a cup of tea?

AIMEE (*uncertainly*). Em...

TOMMY. It's no problem. I'm having one.

AIMEE. Okay. Thanks.

She goes into the loo and shuts the door. TOMMY *checks the kettle and flicks the switch. He looks for some mugs. There are no clean ones. He picks one up from the floor and sniffs it, it seems acceptable. He rinses their mugs in the sink and throws two teabags into them. He quickly shoves some used takeaway containers and dirty work-clothes away. He tidies up to make some space as best he can. He piles some newspapers on top of others, mostly copies of the* Evening Herald, *but they cascade on to the floor again. At a loss, he kicks them in under the bed.* AIMEE *comes out.*

TOMMY. Okay?

AIMEE *nods.*

I'm sorry about that loo. It's just one that I use. The one on the landing is for the whole house but it's always freezing.

AIMEE. Is there many people?

TOMMY. No, only my Uncle Maurice. It's his house. He lives upstairs. (*Pause.*) There's another lad who kips in here with me sometimes if we have an early start, 'cause he gives me a hand with the van. Did you see that van outside? White Datsun Urvan?

AIMEE. No, I...

TOMMY. That's my van.

TOMMY *goes to pour hot water in their cups.* AIMEE *looks down at some books on the camp bed.*

Do you like Westerns? You can have all of them. (*Short pause.*) I've been meaning to drop them up to the Vincent de Paul but I'm just so busy. Do you take sugar?

AIMEE. Thanks.

> TOMMY *brings* AIMEE*'s tea and a bag of sugar to her,*
> *finding something to put it down on.*

TOMMY. Spoon's in the bag.

AIMEE. Thanks.

> TOMMY *gets his tea and watches her spoon a few spoonfuls*
> *into her cup. They are silent for a moment.*

TOMMY. There's milks in the bag.

> *He gestures to a bag of UHT miniatures on the table.*

> I'll tell you one thing. You were extremely lucky.

AIMEE. Yeah?

TOMMY. Yeah! 'Cause I bumped into this fucking eejit on my
way out of Joyce's who said he owed me a pint – I didn't
know who he was. But you see I was starving. I'd been
promising myself a bag of chips, so… (*Signals with his*
thumb: 'I left.') Only for that I wouldn't even have seen what
happened you.

AIMEE. Yeah, well…

TOMMY. Yeah! Split-second timing. (*Pause.*) And I dropped
my bleeding chips. In the end. (*Short pause.*) Somewhere.

AIMEE. I'm sorry.

TOMMY. Who was he? Boyfriend?

AIMEE. No.

TOMMY (*unconvinced*). Yeah?

AIMEE. Just someone giving me a lift.

TOMMY. Do you know him well?

AIMEE. No.

TOMMY. Well, this is it. There you go. You can't just get in a
car with fellas you don't know. You know? I mean,
unfortunately, that's… but there you are.

AIMEE. I don't know you and I'm in your flat.

Short pause.

TOMMY. But that's different.

AIMEE. How is it different?

TOMMY. It's different because I'm different.

AIMEE. Different to what?

TOMMY. What do you mean 'different to what'? Different to fellas like him.

AIMEE. Yeah?

TOMMY. Yeah! Listen. I've never hit a woman in my whole life – ever. And listen, believe me there was times I had good reason to. Very good reason to. Maybe I fucking should have!

AIMEE. Okay.

Pause.

TOMMY. Yeah. (*Short pause.*) I can't believe you'd compare me to someone like him.

AIMEE. I never said that.

Pause.

TOMMY. Do you want a biscuit?

AIMEE. No thanks.

TOMMY. I'm starving.

TOMMY *goes to get himself a biscuit.*

So what did he hit you for?

AIMEE. I don't know, 'cause I was trying to make a phone call I think.

TOMMY. A phone call?

AIMEE. Yeah, he grabbed my phone and he pulled over. I thought he was just gonna let me out but…

TOMMY. Yeah I saw him! Only he heard me shouting… I mean… (*Shakes his head, indicating how much worse it could have been.*) I got his reg. 09 D something something.

AIMEE. It's just a phone.

TOMMY. Yeah, I suppose. Do you need to call anyone? Unfortunately I have no credit but Uncle Maurice would probably let us use his landline, if you want me to wake him.

AIMEE. No it's alright.

TOMMY. Are you sure?

AIMEE. Yeah, it's okay, really. Thanks.

TOMMY. He might only go mad if I woke him up now anyway.

He looks at AIMEE, *watching her stare into her cup.*

Do you want to stay here?

She looks at him. Pause.

AIMEE. Where?

TOMMY. In the camp bed. Or over here and I can kip in the front room, Maurice won't mind. I mean, if that's… if you want to get a taxi, I'd give you the money only I don't… (*Looks at some change from his pocket.*) Or I could drop you somewhere, it's no problem.

AIMEE *looks at the camp bed.*

Or you can sleep there. The other pile of books is all James Bond.

The lights change while music/sound fades up. When the change is complete, AIMEE *is gone.* TOMMY *stands, one side of his face covered in shaving foam, razor in hand, while he talks on a hands-free earpiece. He is in his shirt, underwear and socks. The music fades into a little transistor radio. Morning light reveals the room's true squalor. It is the next day.*

Well, I don't know what happened to it then. It was in a little yellow envelope. Doc stuck it in the letter box. (*Pause.*)

Yeah. Three hundred euros. Suzanne, give me some credit, will you? (*Pause.*) Well, one of the kids must have picked it up. Ask them. (*Pause.*) Michelle? Yeah, of course I'll meet her. Listen, I went to meet her the last time she didn't even show up I was left standing there freezing my arse off on North Earl Street. (*Pause.*) Well, that might be what she says but it was her who stood me up. (*Pause.*) Oh? (*Pause.*) What does her teacher say? (*Pause.*) Well, if she's better off out of school, well then, that's... What do you mean? I do care! Of course I care! I will, I'll text her now if you get off the bleeding phone. Yeah, I'll meet up with her. Listen, I'm happy to talk to her if she'll talk to me...

TOMMY *is startled by a noise, he turns to see a man in his forties come through the double doors from the garden balcony. He wears a sweater, glasses, a woollen hat and filthy-looking trousers. This is* TOMMY*'s friend and business associate,* DOC. *He is carrying a dirty sack.*

Yeah, I have to go. I'll call you later. Okay. I will! Bye. (*Hangs up.*) For Jaysus' sake, Doc!

DOC (*his usual greeting*). Aye aye.

TOMMY *goes to resume shaving over at the little mirror above the sink.*

TOMMY. Why do you always have to come in the bleeding window? Giving me a heart attack.

DOC. 'Cause then I wouldn't have got all of these out of Maurice's vegetable patch.

TOMMY (*rounds on him*). I told you not to be doing that! He thinks it's me!

DOC (*pulling a turnip out of the sack*). Yeah, but look at that turnip – look at it! You're not looking at it!

TOMMY. You're a fucking turnip! You're getting muck all over the floor!

DOC (*producing more vegetables*). And the potatoes are absolutely perfect. He'll just let them all rot in the ground!

TOMMY. Well, that's his business! And you fucking nicking them in broad daylight – he'll be straight down in here now in a minute!

DOC. His curtains were closed.

TOMMY. Right...

DOC. You can't see through the hedge, Tommy. Trust me, I know what I'm doing.

TOMMY. What did you do? Climb over the wall?

DOC. Don't have to, the back gate is busted, you just push it.

TOMMY *finds his trousers and gets dressed.*

TOMMY. Yeah, well, as soon as I get my tools out of the lock-up, all that'll be over, mate. And listen, don't you think for a second you're gonna be boiling any of that crap up in here. He'll be down like a bullet.

DOC. We'll just say we bought it, Tommy. Chillax, will you? I'll stick 'em in under here, no one'll be any the wiser. (*Pushes the sack in under the camp bed and pushes some books in around it. Finds a bloody tissue on the bed.*) Hey, did you cut yourself shaving?

TOMMY. What? Yeah. Here stick that in the bin, will you?

DOC *considers all the black plastic bags.*

DOC. Which one's the bin?

TOMMY. Any of them.

DOC (*getting rid of tissue*). So listen, Tommy, any chance of me getting my wages today?

TOMMY. Wages? For what?

DOC. Thirty euros.

TOMMY. Thirty euros?!

DOC. Yeah – for those two days we did last week.

TOMMY. What two days?

DOC. On Monday we picked up all those Peppa Pig potties in County Meath.

TOMMY. What Peppa Pig potties?

DOC. The Peppa Pig potties! And last Thursday when we cleaned out the lock-up.

TOMMY. Cleaning out the lock-up doesn't count as a day, Doc, come on.

DOC. It was nearly dark by the time we took everything out – we had to just put it all back because we couldn't see anything!

TOMMY. Yeah, in a whole new system. Though.

DOC. Listen, we didn't get out of there till nearly eight o'clock, Tommy. So two days, fifteen euros a day, thirty euros.

TOMMY. Yeah, but wait, hold on – I bought you your lunch the day we went out to County Meath.

DOC. No you didn't!

TOMMY. I did!

DOC. You didn't! You gave me a half of your banana sandwich when we were sitting in that traffic jam in Mullingar!

TOMMY. Yeah? And?

DOC. Ah come on, Tommy…

TOMMY. That was your lunch! What do you want?

DOC. You said we were gonna go to a carvery!

TOMMY. Yeah, well, I carved the banana!

DOC. Don't give me that…

TOMMY. We had no time for a carvery! The traffic was murder, Doc!

DOC. Tommy, you owe me thirty squids. End of. Don't be so stingy.

TOMMY. Wait a minute! Wait a minute! Wait a minute! Who's stingy? Have I ever let you down?

DOC. No. That's what I'm… that's what I'm saying.

TOMMY. This is just the art of negotiation, Doc. This is how you learn it.

DOC. Yeah I know.

TOMMY. Of course I'm gonna pay you. What do you think I am, for Jaysus' sake? And just to show you there's no hard feelings, you know what I'm gonna do?

TOMMY *goes to a pile of crap and digs out three boxes of cigars*.

DOC. Ah, Tommy, not the cigars!

TOMMY. No, no, no wait listen, listen… You know how much these cigars retail for, in any of the fancy shops in town? Seven euros each!

DOC (*simultaneously with* TOMMY).…Seven euros each…

TOMMY. Yes, bang on! Seven euros each. There's twenty cigars in each of these boxes. Do the maths. Go on, do it.

DOC. Eh…

TOMMY. Straight retail? Sixty cigars?

DOC. Yeah…

TOMMY. Yeah, what is it?

DOC. Yeah, it's…

TOMMY. Seven by twenty, by three.

DOC. Yeah…

TOMMY. That's right. One forty, by three, how much is that?

DOC. Yeah…

TOMMY. That's right. Four hundred and twenty euros, straight retail, with all your taxes and overheads and all that bollocks all thrown in – but the beauty of this? As a business model? You *have* no overheads, or tax, you just walk into Joyce's bar on any night of the week – at your leisure – whip these out, a euro a piece, two euros a pop, and you've already doubled your money. Because? (*Handing the boxes to* DOC.) Because why?

DOC. Yeah.

TOMMY. Because that's… you're a good businessman. Or are you not a good businessman?

DOC. No, I am a good businessman.

TOMMY. Well, there you go. And that's all on me. Whatever profit you make. That's yours. I don't ask for a cent.

DOC. Yeah, but you know these are all out of date…

TOMMY. In what sense?

DOC. The date on the box.

TOMMY. On that? Don't mind that! That's just we have to follow EU regulations – they have to have a stamp on it because there's tobacco in it – but you ask any connoisseur – cigars never go out of date.

DOC. They do. They dry out.

TOMMY. Drying out only makes them easier to light. Everybody says that.

DOC. Well, even so, look, thanks, Tommy, but I can't sell them in Joyce's, so…

TOMMY. Why not?

DOC (*putting the cigar boxes back in* TOMMY*'s trunk*). The new lad who works on the door won't let me in any more.

TOMMY. Why?

DOC. He says I'm not a regular.

TOMMY. You are a regular. You're very regular.

DOC. That's what I said but your man says he doesn't care how regular I say I am, I'm not as regular as the other regulars.

TOMMY. Yes you are!

DOC. Yeah, well, the other regulars are more regular, and he says it doesn't matter how regular I ever become – I'll never be as regular a regular as the other regulars because they're just way more, eh...

TOMMY. Regular?

DOC. Yeah.

TOMMY. Well, sell them in the Padraig Pearse!

DOC. I'm barred out of the Padraig Pearse!

TOMMY. Since when?!

DOC. Since I went in trying to sell all that black pudding you gave me! Your man in there whipped out a baseball bat and chased me all out into the car park – I fell down an open manhole and he just broke his shite laughing at me!

TOMMY. So what do you want me to do about it?

DOC. What?

TOMMY. Well, like that's just not my problem, Doc.

DOC. Tommy, listen to me, all I'm saying is, no cigars, no black pudding, no banana sandwiches, you owe me thirty euros, Tommy, end of story, sin scéal eile, that's it!

TOMMY. Alright! Keep your wig on, Doc! All you had to do was say that! Jaysus! What do you want – cash or a cheque?

DOC. Yes, cash.

TOMMY. Cash won't be a problem. (*As though* DOC *has behaved completely unreasonably*.) It's alright. Everything's okay...

TOMMY *goes to a loose floorboard and lifts it, taking out a little biscuit tin. He opens it and counts out some five-euro notes.*

Now, twenty euros, cash, count it.

DOC. Thirty euros.

TOMMY. That's what I mean. Thirty euros. Count it.

DOC. This is only twenty euros.

TOMMY. Count it!

DOC. I am counting it! It's twenty euros.

TOMMY. Exactly! (*Handing over another pair of five-euro notes*.) Now count the rest of it.

DOC. And listen, I haven't forgotten my Christmas money you know.

TOMMY. That money is beyond question, Doc. I'm holding it for you right here. I'll have it for you at Christmas, you just say the word. I mean otherwise…

DOC. Yeah, I know, I'm just…

TOMMY. Roll around Christmas, Doc is broke.

DOC. No, I'm just saying it, so, our accounts are in order.

TOMMY. Our accounts are in impeccable order, Doc. As you well know, I challenged, I *dared*, the revenue commissioners to come and audit me, you know that. They ran a bleeding mile, so they did, because they were terrified – of our accounts!

TOMMY *is putting the biscuit tin back under the floorboard as* AIMEE *appears in the doorway, holding a towel round her head.* TOMMY *quickly conceals what he is doing.*

You alright?

AIMEE. Does the water just go cold like that?

TOMMY. Oh yeah, you get about five minutes and then…

(*Indicating upstairs.*) 'Cause Maurice only ever puts on the small immersion. (*As* AIMEE *turns to go.*) If you want to wait for another few minutes then you can… (*Again,* AIMEE *is about to go.*) Sorry, this is Doc.

DOC. Hello.

AIMEE. Hi.

> AIMEE *once again looks towards the door.*

TOMMY. This is… Aimee.

> DOC *just stares at* AIMEE.

DOC. Hello.

> AIMEE *sits on the bed. Silence, until* TOMMY *stands, followed by* DOC *and* AIMEE.

TOMMY. So, look, we're gonna go out. We have to do a few bits and pieces and we'll… We'll be back.

AIMEE. Is there any deodorant I could use?

TOMMY (*looks around*). Deodorant, deodorant. Doc, do you see any deodorant there?

DOC. Deodorant? Deodorant?

TOMMY (*finds some*). Oh look.

AIMEE (*not wanting to be rude*). Oh thanks, Old Spice…

TOMMY (*laughs*). Yeah, well, I'm not… I'm hardly gonna have a woman's deodorant, am I? Although… (*Suddenly goes and rummages in a box.*) I mean… (*Looks around.*) I might…

> DOC *stands looking at* AIMEE. *He produces a packet of peanuts and offers her one.*

AIMEE (*taking a peanut*). Thank you. Are you a doctor?

DOC. A doctor? No. Why?

AIMEE. He called you Doc.

DOC. No, it's, it's just short for Brian.

AIMEE. How is Doc short for Brian?

DOC. Well, I used to be called Bri – short for Brian – but then, em…

AIMEE. But why would you need to make Brian any shorter?

DOC. Ah, it's a bit long.

AIMEE. You can't get much shorter than Brian.

DOC. No, Aimee, I'm afraid that's where you're wrong there, because, you see, you can. Bri is actually two letters shorter. Than Brian.

AIMEE. But it nearly takes longer to say Bri than Brian though, doesn't it?

DOC. Well, that's why it got shortened again – to Doc. I mean, people don't have all day to be saying your name, you know what I mean?

AIMEE. But how do you get Doc out of Brian?

TOMMY (*from the toilet, still rooting*). Doc Martens.

AIMEE. Is your second name Martens?

DOC. No, my name is Brian de Burca, but I used to always wear Doc Martens so…

TOMMY (*still in the toilet*). He has fallen arches.

DOC. Yeah, so people used always call me 'Docs'.

AIMEE. Okay.

DOC. But that was a bit long so…

AIMEE. Right.

DOC. So now it's just – (*Indicates straight ahead.*) Doc.

TOMMY *has emerged from toilet still looking for the deodorant.*

TOMMY. Doc works with me and he… he's my associate in our business and he…

DOC. I sometimes sleep in the camp bed.

TOMMY…. Yeah. The odd time. If we have an early start.

DOC. But I'm basically freelance.

TOMMY. Yeah.

DOC. By definition.

TOMMY. Yeah. We both are.

AIMEE sits on the bed sorting her laundry, which TOMMY *has left there, tangled up with his.*

DOC. Because technically I'm actually disabled so I shouldn't be working – at all.

TOMMY. No.

DOC. But I want to work.

TOMMY. He likes to work.

AIMEE. You don't look very disabled.

DOC. Well, thank you for saying that. But unfortunately, I'm afraid I am.

AIMEE. What's your disability?

TOMMY. Well, Aimee, Doc has a mild, I mean it's very mild, but he actually has a mild learning disability? (*Beat.*) Believe it or not.

AIMEE. Okay.

TOMMY. But he's very mild. He's borderline.

DOC. It's borderline.

TOMMY. I mean, the way the doctor put it was like this: apparently no matter how long Doc may have to process unfolding… events at any present given time he will always, *always*, be five to ten minutes behind everybody else.

DOC. Five to seven minutes.

TOMMY. Five to seven minutes, excuse me.

DOC. I mean, I get there!

TOMMY. Oh he gets there!

DOC. I get there in the end. Just…

Short pause.

TOMMY. About fifteen minutes after everybody else.

DOC *shrugs as though saying 'I can handle it.'*

But Doc is very brave, and he's actually very talented...

DOC. It's just with new things.

TOMMY. Just new things. That's all.

AIMEE. Right.

TOMMY. Yeah, so...

Pause.

DOC. And how are you?

AIMEE. Yeah, I'm... I'm fine thank you.

TOMMY (*finds a deodorant spray in a box*). Aha! Lynx. That do you?

AIMEE. Yeah, no, that's fine.

TOMMY. But look I'll tell you what, we're gonna head out to get you some shampoo and anything else, what else do you need?

AIMEE. You don't have to do that.

TOMMY. No, it's no problem. We probably have... we always have a bit of everything at the lock-up.

AIMEE. Well, thanks I'll just... I'll try the water again, 'cause I just need to rinse my hair, so...

TOMMY. Should be some there now. Now, Aimee, there's beans over here. Tea, coffee, crackers. Don't eat them dog biscuits.

DOC. Do you like turnips?

AIMEE. Em...

TOMMY. Doc...

DOC (*conspiratorially*). Listen, there's a bag of turnips in under there.

TOMMY. She's not gonna be boiling up turnips, you bleeding dingbat, leave her alone. Now the only thing, Aimee, when you're done, just stay in here. Uncle Maurice can be bit... he's alright, but he can just be a bit... 'Who's in the house?' You know what I mean?

AIMEE. Okay.

TOMMY. Just fucking stay in here we'll be back in an hour and we'll get you sorted out, alright?

AIMEE. Okay. Thanks, Tommy.

AIMEE *goes*. TOMMY *breezily acts as though nothing unusual is happening*.

TOMMY. Right, where's me keys?

TOMMY *starts looking through jackets and pockets for his keys*.

DOC. Who is that?

TOMMY. Who? Aimee?

DOC. Yeah. I know her.

TOMMY. Yeah? From where?

DOC. I don't know. It'll come back to me.

TOMMY. Yeah, well, she's just kipping here for a few nights. She was in a spot of bother.

DOC. She's kipping in here?

TOMMY. She was in the camp bed. I was in the front room.

DOC. And Maurice doesn't know?

TOMMY. Why should he know? This is my place in here, so...

DOC. So where will I kip?

TOMMY. When?

DOC. Tonight?

TOMMY. What are you talking about?

TOMMY *has retrieved the hammer and is using it to free the euro from the meter once again.*

DOC. I told you my sister says I can't keep going back there. She says her boyfriend is going to piss off on her 'cause I'm always in her toilet.

TOMMY. Well, now, Doc, that's not really my problem, in fairness now, is it?

DOC. I'll sleep in the front room with you.

TOMMY. There's only the old settee in there, there's nothing else to sleep on.

DOC. I'll bring in the camp bed.

TOMMY. Aimee is in the camp bed.

DOC. But she can sleep in your bed.

TOMMY. Yeah, but that's my bed, Doc, you know what I mean? She's in the camp bed.

DOC. I'll sleep in the van.

TOMMY. Ah come on, Doc.

DOC. No, I like sleeping in the van, you know that.

TOMMY. But that's gonna be a pain in the hole! If the guards twig you're sleeping in the van again, they'll go apeshit... Just tell your sister you'll stay out of her way and it's only for a few nights while Aimee is here, 'cause she's afraid to go out.

DOC *is staring out the double doors at the trees in the park.*

Doc. Alright? Doc. (*Pause.*) Doc. Alright? Come on, let's go. (*Pause.*) Alright! Sleep in the fucking van, okay? You can sleep in the van. Alright? Come on. Let's go. (*Pause.*) What's the matter with you?!

DOC. No... I... just remembered. I know where I know her from.

TOMMY. Who, Aimee?

DOC. Yeah. Fintan Mackenacky pointed her out to me one night down in Joyce's bar last Christmas. He said she's on the game.

TOMMY. He said that about Aimee?

DOC. Yeah. He said she pulled him off in his back garden for forty euros on the previous October bank holiday.

TOMMY. His back garden? Come on...

DOC. No I swear to God.

TOMMY. Listen, Doc, I don't want that kind of talk in here, alright?

DOC. What?

TOMMY. I said I don't like that kind of talk.

DOC. Oh, yeah. Okay. Sorry, Tommy.

Pause.

TOMMY. And that's probably fucking bullshit anyway. I mean, what would Fintan Mackenacky know? The cross-eyed fucking head on him – can he even see properly? You know what I mean? Fucking – (*Weaves his head around.*) one eye going that way and the other one kind of coming around trying to look at you – you know what I mean?

DOC *bursts out laughing but stops when the door opens. MAURICE enters, stick in hand, a white shirt and an old blazer on. He carries a piece of paper.*

Would you not ever think of not knocking? No?

MAURICE. Why should I?

TOMMY. Because this is where I live!

MAURICE. Yeah, in my house!

TOMMY. And this is my flat!

MAURICE. You call this a flat?

TOMMY. What would you call it?

MAURICE. A room in my house.

TOMMY. That I pay rent in.

MAURICE. Yeah, chance would be a fine thing! And where's my paper?

TOMMY *goes towards the toilet to get it.*

TOMMY. I was just bringing it up to you.

MAURICE. Yeah well, you can just leave it where it lands on the doormat in future, thanks, I can get it myself. And there's the other genius.

DOC. There I am. Well, Maurice. What think ye of Christ?

MAURICE. What?

DOC. How's it going?

MAURICE. Yeah.

DOC. You're looking well anyway. Is someone else doing your hair for you these days?

MAURICE. Would you go away of that and don't be annoying me.

TOMMY (*bringing the extremely read-looking paper out from the toilet to* MAURICE). Here, I was saving your legs for you.

MAURICE (*unimpressed*). Yeah, sure… Look at it!

Behind MAURICE*'s back,* TOMMY *signals to* DOC *that they should go.*

And here, who's used all the hot water?

TOMMY. I was using it to have a shave. Is that alright?

MAURICE. What were you shaving? A dog? There's no water left!

TOMMY. Well, if you're only gonna put the immersion on for two minutes a day, Maurice, you can hardly expect…

MAURICE. What in the name of God would you know about the immersion, or what it costs for that matter?

TOMMY. Listen, mate, that meter up there is chock-a-block full of money I have to keep putting in and taking out – and all I ever use is – (*Pointing.*) that kettle for a cup of tea or – (*Pointing.*) them two lamps so I'm not sitting in here in the dark! Now if you will please excuse us, we have work to do, actually, alright?

At TOMMY*'s signal,* TOMMY *and* DOC *start to go.*

MAURICE. The guards were looking for you.

TOMMY. What?

MAURICE. The police.

TOMMY. When?

MAURICE. Yesterday afternoon. Two detectives called saying your van was caught on CCTV when you drove off without paying for petrol at a station in Enfield in County Kildare last week.

TOMMY. Last week?

MAURICE. Yep.

TOMMY. *Last* week? Well, I am flummoxed by this 'cause that can't have been em…

MAURICE. They gave me a picture. It's your van with your registration.

MAURICE *hands* TOMMY *a printout of the picture.*

TOMMY. You do know Enfield is not in County Kildare, it's in County Meath?

MAURICE. What's that got to do with it?

TOMMY. No, I'm just saying. I wonder if they know, 'cause…

MAURICE. Well, if you want to tell them where this misunderstanding actually occurred, his number is on there.

TOMMY. Yeah well, look, that's no problem. (*A sickened laugh.*) You know what that was?

MAURICE. What?

TOMMY. Doc, do you remember? You were gonna… and I was gonna… and then you had gone back in for a Twix or something

DOC. I went back in for a Twix.

TOMMY. And I thought… (*Signalling to* MAURICE *that* DOC *is useless.*) You fucking eejit!

DOC. Yeah…

MAURICE. Well, that's fine then, isn't it?

TOMMY. Yeah! We'll get that sorted out. (*Short pause.*) Right, well look, do you want a lift to the shops?

MAURICE. No, I've been to the shops.

TOMMY. Oh, okay. Well. I might lock up here actually so…

MAURICE. Well, if you don't mind I was going to do a landlord's inspection.

TOMMY. A what?

MAURICE. You actually think I could face looking through all this crap? No, I just wanted to remind you about Maura's anniversary mass on Saturday.

TOMMY. Oh yeah.

MAURICE. You're going to it.

TOMMY. Oh yeah, no that's…

MAURICE. Ten o'clock.

TOMMY. Yeah.

MAURICE. Alright, well, I'll see you later.

TOMMY. Right.

MAURICE *goes to the double doors and looks down into the garden.* TOMMY *loiters at the door for a moment wondering if he should just bite the bullet and tell* MAURICE *about* AIMEE.

Listen, Maurice…

MAURICE. What.

Pause.

TOMMY. Don't let yourself get too cold. (*Pause.*) Okay well… I'll see you later.

MAURICE. Mind how you go.

TOMMY *and* DOC *leave, going off, through the double doors.* MAURICE *inspects the electricity meter. After a few moments he calls out.*

You can come in. You don't have to hide out there in the hallway.

Pause. AIMEE *appears in the doorway.*

And you are…?

AIMEE. Aimee Clement. You Uncle Maurice?

MAURICE. The very same. (*Roots in his pocket.*) Come here, Aimee Clement, I want you to climb up there to that box for me.

MAURICE *holds a little key out to her.*

AIMEE. What do I do?

MAURICE. You open it and pull out the drawer.

AIMEE *climbs up on a chair and opens the electricity meter.*

You didn't see anyone bringing any fresh vegetables up through here, did you?

AIMEE. What?

MAURICE. Never mind, show me that.

AIMEE *hands him down the drawer. He takes out a single coin.*

Now what would you make of this?

AIMEE. I'd say someone is just putting the same coin in it over and over.

MAURICE (*ironically*). Oh, you think? Here, put it back.

He throws the coin back in the drawer and AIMEE *slides it back to the meter.*

How long have you been here?

AIMEE. Since last night.

MAURICE. How long are you staying?

AIMEE. I don't know. Not long.

MAURICE. So, what, you're a friend of Tommy's?

AIMEE. I suppose.

MAURICE. You know he's married?

AIMEE. He told me he's been living here for two years so I don't know how married that makes him.

MAURICE. Married is married.

AIMEE. You married?

MAURICE. My wife slipped on the ice outside the gate there, three years ago, got a clot on the brain that no one detected. Passed ten days later.

Pause.

AIMEE. Do you have kids?

MAURICE (*shakes his head*). We used to look after Tommy, you see. And now I'm still bleeding looking after him!

AIMEE *smiles.*

Yeah! (*Pause.*) So… You gonna tell me anything about yourself?

AIMEE. Nothing to tell.

MAURICE. I doubt that somehow. You married?

AIMEE. No.

MAURICE. Kids?

AIMEE (*a tiny hesitation*). No.

MAURICE. Do you take drugs?

AIMEE. No.

MAURICE. Yeah? (*Pause.*) I can't have any trouble. And Tommy doesn't need any trouble. (*Pause.*) Alright?

AIMEE *nods.*

Do you want some breakfast?

AIMEE *looks around at* TOMMY*'s filthy food station.*

AIMEE. Well…

MAURICE. You can't eat in here! Come up to me in ten minutes, you can have a boiled egg that won't give you botulism.

MAURICE *goes.* AIMEE *stands there. The lights change, dusk falling to night until all is dark except for external light through the windows and a little night light from somewhere off in the house. Silence as though no one is there. Then we hear* AIMEE *crying out in the darkness; then* TOMMY*'s voice calling out in startled reaction to hers. He flicks on a lamp. We can see that* TOMMY *and* AIMEE *are in bed together.* AIMEE *is having a nightmare.* TOMMY *shakes her awake.*

TOMMY. Hey! Hey! Hey! It's alright! Aimee! You're dreaming! You're dreaming…

AIMEE *looks about, unsure where she is for a moment. She sits up. A loud thumping noise comes from upstairs.*

AIMEE. What's that?

TOMMY. It's Maurice. (*Calls out*.) Alright, Maurice! It's alright!

The thumping stops.

He hates noise. Are you alright?

He reaches out and looks at his watch.

AIMEE. What time is it?

TOMMY. Eleven. Are you okay?

AIMEE. Yeah.

TOMMY. Here, do you want another drink?

TOMMY *gets out of bed, wearing a T-shirt and boxers. He pours some rum into a couple of mugs and brings them to the bed. He hands her one and stands looking down at her. He blows through his lips.*

Some dream.

AIMEE. Yeah.

TOMMY. What were you dreaming about?

AIMEE. We were somewhere. We were…

TOMMY. Who?

AIMEE. You and me. We were in here and two men came in and told me I was dead and I had to get up and go with them. And it was like… (*Shudders*.) uh!

TOMMY. Jaysus, well, you nearly gave me a heart attack.

They laugh.

Are you hungry?

AIMEE (*still waking up*). Em…

TOMMY. I didn't know I'd fallen asleep.

AIMEE. Me neither.

Pause.

TOMMY. That was… em… That was… (*Points at the bed.*)
That was A-one.

AIMEE. Oh. Good.

TOMMY. A-one. Excellent.

AIMEE. Okay.

TOMMY. I mean this… this suits me… (*Getting his trousers
and taking some money out.*) Forty right?

She nods. He puts it on the locker.

And I'll tell you why – because… in a… in a *relationship*…
you have all this fucking… *negotiation* and everything.
Whereas, this way: that's your money. That's… everything is
– (*Indicates 'on the level'.*)

AIMEE (*indicates money*). Well look, if you prefer to call that
the rent and…

TOMMY. The rent! Don't mind the rent! What are you talking
about? That's… (*Indicates money.*) That's… (*Indicates
'yours'.*)

AIMEE. That's all I ever do, okay?

TOMMY. But that's perfect! That's all I would ever… I mean…
the full… the full job and all that huffing and puffing, it's so
unbecoming. But the hand. The hand is perfect. It's a service,
I mean, it's a skill, don't get me wrong. I'd take care of
myself only – (*Rubs his elbow.*) I have repetitive strain
injury. But that was – that was absolutely A-one. I must
have… I passed out!

AIMEE *smiles. They take a sip from their drinks.*

So look, no bullshit now. The man who hit you. Was that…
Was he like… a…

AIMEE. No, he was my boyfriend.

TOMMY. I knew it! Didn't I say that to you?

AIMEE. Well, my ex.

TOMMY. I fucking hope he was your ex! Jaysus!

AIMEE. Yeah.

TOMMY. You're well shot of him.

AIMEE. I know.

TOMMY. Yeah. You're well shot of him now. Okay?

Short pause.

Here. I got you a coat.

He gets an overcoat and brings it to her. It is an old dark grey Crombie.

AIMEE. Thanks.

TOMMY. I don't know if it's for a man or a woman. I don't think it matters…

AIMEE *takes it and tries it on.*

…with this kind of coat.

It looks good on her. TOMMY *nods his approval.*

AIMEE. Thanks, Tommy.

TOMMY. I mean, it'll do you, just in the cold, so you're not…

AIMEE. No, it's really cool. Thanks.

TOMMY. I'll get you a few more bits and pieces.

AIMEE *darts to a spot and pulls out a pair of runners wrapped in a towel. She brings them to* TOMMY. *The runners are huge, certainly too big for* TOMMY.

What's this?

AIMEE. I was round in that shopping centre round there.

TOMMY. Yeah?

AIMEE. Yeah, I wanted a pair in my size but… that was all I could get.

TOMMY (*looking at the size*). Size fourteen.

AIMEE. Yeah…

TOMMY. They're nice! I could jam a bit of toilet roll up in the toes.

AIMEE. Yeah?

TOMMY. Yeah. Give it a go anyway. Thanks. Thanks for thinking of me. You didn't get a receipt?

Short pause.

AIMEE. No.

TOMMY. I'll stick a bit of toilet roll up 'em. They're very trendy, aren't they?

TOMMY *starts to try the runners.* AIMEE *goes into the toilet and washes her hands.*

AIMEE. How old are your kids?

TOMMY (*dismissively*). Ah! Sixteen and seventeen.

AIMEE. Boys or girls?

TOMMY. The older one is a girl, the other fella's a boy. (*Pause.*) Their mother has turned them against me you see. Brought my daughter a Connemara pony for her birthday there. But I didn't know them fucking things are half-wild, living out the back garden! It kicked in the coal-shed door and knocked down the wall into the fucking neighbours and everything…

AIMEE *laughs.*

Yeah so, no matter what you do, you fucking [mess up somehow]…

Pause.

And then I lost my business and [that was the end of it]…

AIMEE. What do you do?

TOMMY. Ah no, I had two outdoor live-gig rigs? But they got impounded by the department of the social environment

because – even on very calm days – they both kept getting
struck by lightning. I bought them in from Belarus. The bank
threw the money at me! And now it's all like a legal
nightmare and I... (*Suddenly*.) How can you be with a fella
like that? Who hits you and...

Pause.

AIMEE. He changed.

TOMMY (*sceptical, dismissive*). Yeah?

AIMEE. And sometimes... like... if you know that you can kill
yourself... (*Shrugs. Pause*.) I know it sounds mad...

Pause. TOMMY *shrugs.*

TOMMY (*rationally*). Yeah. (*Pause*.) You wouldn't be too
scared. To do it.

AIMEE. I probably would.

TOMMY. Mm.

AIMEE. It's fucking ridiculous.

TOMMY. Yeah. No, listen. I've thought about it.

AIMEE. Yeah?

TOMMY. Yeah. I've thought about it a lot.

AIMEE. Yeah?

TOMMY. Me? I'd just do it with pills. Just... bang. No need to
make a big bleeding point about it. You know? But then you
think, 'What about the other people...'

AIMEE. Yeah.

TOMMY. That's the... What if they need you? You know?
(*Beat*.) They probably don't. I got involved in a boxing match
one time. When I was younger. I was offered five hundred
quid to box a chap over in Wolverhampton. I was never any
use, but I thought – hey, I could win this. Outlook, you see?

AIMEE. What happened?

TOMMY. Ah, he fucking destroyed me. But then afterwards, I'm lying on me back in the dressing room. In he walks, this big black lad, to see if I was gonna be alright. And he's wearing a beautiful suit! Shakes my hand, being real nice to me, and all I could I think about was, 'He brought a fucking suit to the boxing match!' I'd thought I'd had a chance – but you don't bring your suit to wear home unless you *know* you're gonna win, you know what I mean?

They laugh.

Outlook. That's… It's all about your outlook. (*Starts taking off the runners.*) Although – someone told me later, it was probably a fix.

AIMEE *nods thoughtfully. They are startled by the double doors from the balcony rattling and opening with a thump.* TOMMY *wheels around as* DOC's *head peeps in. He wears a bobble hat and carries a bag from the chip shop. He has a nasty-looking black eye.*

DOC. *Guten Nacht mein schitz.*

TOMMY. What are you doing?

DOC. What?

TOMMY (*getting his trousers on*). What do you mean, 'What?' What are you doing?

DOC. Can I come in?

TOMMY. What do you want?

DOC. I have chips.

TOMMY. Do you know what time it is?

DOC. I thought youse might be hungry.

TOMMY. Are you having me on?

DOC. Oh, were youse asleep?

TOMMY. Yeah, well no actually Aimee was asleep, I only came in to get… a… get some milk, and you're after scaring the living daylights out of her here.

DOC. Oh I'm sorry.

TOMMY. Like, I didn't even have me pants on here, Doc!

DOC. No well, I just saw the light and I...

TOMMY. 'Cause I was on my way to bed, like, you know?

DOC. Sorry.

TOMMY. Well, close the bleeding door, will you? You have chips, do you?

DOC. Yeah.

TOMMY. Well, get some plates for fuck's sake.

DOC *goes to the sink, looking for clean plates.*

(*To* AIMEE.) Do you want a few chips?

AIMEE. Yeah.

TOMMY. Get a plate for Aimee, will you? What are you doing? What did you get?

DOC. I got you a smoked cod.

TOMMY. Come here, hold on, what's happened to your face?

DOC (*dismissively*). Ah... Teresa's just pissed off with me staying there.

TOMMY. Did she hit you?

DOC. Nah, her fella gave me a smack. He broke my glasses.

TOMMY. Because you were staying there?

DOC. Well, no because we were all arguing.

TOMMY. It looks nasty.

DOC. Ah, it was more the way he kind of caught me. The strap of his watch kind of... (*Demonstrates the blow.*)

TOMMY. Are you alright?

DOC. Yeah, I'm just starving. Have you got any Sellotape?

TOMMY. Here, let me do that.

> TOMMY *takes over organising the food.* DOC *stands there sheepishly fiddling with his glasses.*

So she threw you out?

DOC. What? Yeah.

TOMMY. This is getting like Jurys Inns here. There you go.

> TOMMY *hands* DOC *a plate.*

DOC. Thanks, Tommy.

TOMMY. Is there a single here for Aimee?

DOC. They always throw in the extra scoop – you'd be mad buying another single!

> TOMMY *signals to* AIMEE, *'Get this guy.'* TOMMY *brings some food to* AIMEE *and they all eat from plates on their laps throughout the following.*

Here I got you a present.

TOMMY. For me?

DOC (*takes out a CD*). *The Rockin' Sound of the Vuvuzela* – double CD for 2.99!

TOMMY. Oh, thanks, Doc.

DOC. And a book for 1.99. We can share it. *How to Survive Life-Threatening Situations.*

TOMMY. That's handy!

DOC. Check it out. Chapter One: Surviving a Gun Attack.

AIMEE. A what attack?

DOC. A gun attack. 'If your assailant is firing directly at you…'

TOMMY. Yeah…

DOC. 'Try to move away.'

TOMMY. Okay.

DOC. 'And as soon as you can…'

TOMMY. Yeah?

DOC. 'Turn a corner.'

Pause.

TOMMY. Is that it?

DOC. 'However should you be unable to turn a corner or are not in a built-up area…'

TOMMY. Yeah.

DOC. 'Locate a large object, such as a motorised vehicle…'

TOMMY. Yeah…

DOC. 'And endeavour to keep it between you and your assailant.'

TOMMY. Okay.

DOC. 'However, should you ascertain that your assailant is discharging armour-piercing ammunition…'

TOMMY. Yeah?

DOC. 'A car will provide little cover.'

TOMMY. No shit.

AIMEE. How do you ascertain if your assailant is discharging armour-piercing ammunition?

DOC. What? The bullets will go through the car, Aimee.

TOMMY. You see?

DOC. They will pierce the armour.

AIMEE. So what do you do?

DOC. What do you do, what?

AIMEE. If your assailant is discharging armour-piercing ammunition?

DOC (*looks at the book*). That's it.

AIMEE. That's all it says?

DOC. Well, you're running out of options in fairness, Aimee. I mean, be realistic, he's got a gun, you know what I mean? Chapter Two: How to Survive an Attack of Killer Wasps.

TOMMY. Well, that's... (*As though he has been there before*.) You do not even want to be *in* that situation!

DOC. No!

TOMMY. Stay out of that one! Do not even get *in* to that one – would be my [advice]...

DOC. Yeah.

They eat their chips for a few moments.

TOMMY. Tell Aimee about your book, Doc.

DOC. It's not a book.

AIMEE. What is it?

DOC. Ah it's just... I write down my dreams and stuff.

TOMMY. Tell Aimee what it's called.

DOC. *The Call of Nature*.

AIMEE *smiles while she eats*.

TOMMY (*to* AIMEE, *playfully*). What?

AIMEE. No, nothing.

DOC. It's just a few pages of a copybook, it's not a book.

TOMMY. Don't be down on yourself. Doc is very spiritual.

DOC. Don't mind him.

TOMMY. Read out that thing you heard on the radio. Doc hears things on the radio.

DOC. Nah, I'm not reading it out.

TOMMY. Tell Aimee what you heard, about the Pope.

DOC. Ah that was... I heard on the news that they were hoping
the Pope was gonna be able to walk from his funeral in the
church down to the graveyard by himself, but then they said
that it didn't look like that was gonna be able to happen.

Short pause.

AIMEE. What?

DOC. Yeah and then the next day – on the news – the Pope was
dead.

TOMMY. What do you make of that?

AIMEE. Yeah, that's... that's insane.

DOC. It's crazy!

TOMMY. And he's a student of Eastern philosophy.

DOC. I'm not really – I just do my yoga in the back of the van.
I used to go to a class but they asked me to stop coming.

AIMEE. Why?

DOC. Because during one class... I actually started to levitate –
just a tiny bit – and everyone got a bit freaked out.

AIMEE. What?!

DOC. No, it's true, I went into a trance and I started to – (*Lifts
himself up a little as though to demonstrate levitation.*) and
this girl starts screaming.

AIMEE. Were you not just dreaming?

DOC (*affronted*). No. Aimee, there was a time when no one
knew what air was.

AIMEE. What what was?

DOC. What air is. No one understood that hearing things was
just our perception of sound waves? So I'm saying – what
about time waves, you know what I mean?

AIMEE. Not really, no.

DOC. Time waves? Just like sound waves – a day will come when we understand what time is and that we can perceive, you know, time waves, waves in time. Vibrations from another time – like why not?

AIMEE. No, I hear you.

DOC. Yeah!

TOMMY. Fucking… 'Time waves…' Here, Doc.

TOMMY *holds his cup towards* DOC. DOC *gets them some drinks.*

DOC (*going to pour drinks*). Where are you from, Aimee?

AIMEE. Clare Hall.

DOC. Out in the countryside?

AIMEE. It's not the countryside.

DOC. It used to be.

AIMEE. A long time ago maybe.

DOC. Oh no. It was. It was right out. Here, Tommy, will I put on *The Midnight Hour*?

TOMMY. Oh, yeah, lash it on there.

DOC *switches on the transistor radio. Marvin Gaye's 'What's Going On?' starts playing.*

Marvin – turn it up.

DOC *turns it up.* TOMMY *gets to his feet and starts grooving around to the music.* DOC *and* AIMEE *laugh.* TOMMY *sings but his grasp of the words is surprisingly rudimentary considering how much the song seems to mean to him. He holds his hand out to* AIMEE*, she takes it and they groove around together.* DOC *also gets up and grooves around on his own. After a couple of minutes they hear* MAURICE *thumping on the ceiling from upstairs.*

(*Calls up.*) Alright! Alright, Maurice!

DOC *turns off the music.*

Old bollocks would give you a pain in your arse. (*Raises his mug to his poster of Marvin Gaye.*) Marvin, you said it there, man. What's goin' on? That is the question. What in the name of Jaysus is goin' on? The man who answers that one will… (*Raises his mug to whoever will answer that question.*)

DOC. What's goin' on?

TOMMY. What the fuck is goin' on? (*Pause.*) Here, did you check the lottery numbers?

DOC. Nah, I didn't buy a ticket this week.

TOMMY. What, did you forget?

DOC. Nah, sure it's only two-point-two million. I wouldn't be bothered in my hole playing for two-point-two million…

TOMMY. What?! Well, I played it. Here we are, we might all be millionaires and we don't even know! (*To* AIMEE.) You want to nip down with me we can check?

AIMEE. Is it far?

TOMMY. No, just down to the Centra. I have to get milk anyway, we can buzz down on my motorbike. Look. You can pick.

He grabs two motorbike helmets, one modern and one old-fashioned, open-faced helmet with goggles.

AIMEE. Well, I'm not wearing that one!

TOMMY. I'll wear that one.

AIMEE. Go on then, give me a sec.

AIMEE *goes into the little toilet. Silence.*

DOC. I'm sorry, Tommy.

TOMMY. For what?

DOC. For crashing in on you.

TOMMY. No, it's grand, I just… I didn't want her getting a fright.

DOC. Yeah, I'm…

TOMMY. Do you want to stay here tonight?

DOC. Really?

TOMMY. Yeah, just… just clear out early and…

DOC. Thanks, Tommy.

TOMMY. Yeah, but here, listen, about that other thing. About what you were saying she'll do for forty euros…

DOC. I don't have forty euros.

TOMMY. Yeah but even if you did.

DOC. I don't.

TOMMY. Yeah, but even if you did. I can't have that kind of shenanigans going on with Maurice upstairs, he'd go mental.

DOC. I don't have forty euros!

TOMMY. That's not the point! Listen to me!

DOC. I'm only just gonna go asleep!

TOMMY. Just don't be annoying her!

DOC. Tommy, come on. You know me. I'm a good guy, come on.

TOMMY. Yeah I know, but I'm just saying…!

DOC. Tommy, I'm not even able to get the horn!

Pause. The toilet door opens and AIMEE *emerges.*

TOMMY. Alright?

AIMEE. Yeah.

TOMMY. Okay. We won't be long.

DOC. Yeah, see you later.

TOMMY (*pointing upstairs*). And no noise alright?

DOC. Yeah, I won't.

DOC *leans on a pot, causing it to fall to the ground making a loud noise.*

TOMMY (*off*). For fuck's sake, Doc!

TOMMY *and* AIMEE *leave.* DOC *starts to tidy up. He puts some plates by the sink and takes a toilet roll into the loo. While he is in there,* KENNETH *steps into the room. He is slim, but strong looking. He wears a grey/beige suit and fawn-coloured slip-on shoes. He stands there for a moment.* DOC *comes out of the toilet to the sink and continues tidying up for a few moments without noticing* KENNETH.

KENNETH. Tommy?

DOC *jumps, crashing dishes into the sink. He stands looking at* KENNETH, *startled.*

DOC. No, I'm Doc.

KENNETH. Where's Tommy?

DOC. He's gone out.

KENNETH. Oh. (*Pause.*) I might just wait then.

Pause.

DOC. Is he expecting you?

KENNETH. I'd say so, yeah.

DOC. Oh, okay.

KENNETH. Is there no one else here?

DOC. No. Just Maurice. (*Pause.*) The man who lives upstairs. (*Pause.*) It's his house. (*Pause.*) He's probably asleep.

Pause.

KENNETH. Okay.

Pause.

DOC. I wouldn't say Tommy will be long. He's just gone to check the Lotto numbers.

KENNETH. Okay, well, I'll wait here then.

Pause.

DOC. Do you want a cup of tea?

KENNETH. Nah, you have one.

DOC. I'm alright.

KENNETH *looks out the window.*

KENNETH. Look at that. You can't see a thing out there.

DOC. No.

KENNETH. The park is like a big black hole.

DOC. Yeah, the trees block it out.

KENNETH. Right, yeah.

Short pause.

DOC. Sometimes you can hear the animals.

Pause. KENNETH *looks at* DOC.

In the zoo.

KENNETH. Do you ever go down in the park at night?

DOC. In the park?

KENNETH. Yeah.

DOC. No.

KENNETH. I don't blame you. Look at it. Jaysus, look at that! (*Picks a hammer up from a pile of stuff.*) I wouldn't want to get a smack off of that would you?

DOC. No.

KENNETH. That would smack your fucking head off!

DOC.… Yeah!

Pause.

KENNETH. You don't be going out there into the park.

DOC. At night-time?

KENNETH. Yeah.

DOC. No.

KENNETH. 'Cause you look like you might. (*Gives a little laugh*.) You know what I mean?

Short pause.

DOC. Not really. No.

KENNETH. No? You do! You look like you'd have no problem wandering in under the trees there.

DOC. No.

KENNETH. Well, there must be something wrong with my eyes then, is there?

DOC. Well, I don't.

Pause. DOC looks around at the sink.

KENNETH. Are you alright?

DOC. Yeah, no I was just [wondering if I should do the dishes]…

KENNETH. Do you want to do the dishes?

DOC. No… I can [do it later]…

KENNETH. Come here, did you hear about that fella that took his winkle out? Up there behind the girls' primary school?

DOC. What?

KENNETH. You don't know who it was, do you?

DOC. No.

Pause.

KENNETH. It wasn't you, was it?

DOC. No.

Pause.

KENNETH. You sure?

DOC. Yeah.

KENNETH. He was up around the back of the primary school. He took out his winkle.

DOC. I don't know anything about it.

KENNETH. You seem very sure of yourself.

DOC. No.

KENNETH. You're not sure?

DOC. No, I mean, I'm…

KENNETH. You're not sure if it was you, or…?

DOC. No, I am…

KENNETH. But you just don't remember…

DOC. No, I do.

KENNETH. You do remember?

DOC. No, it wasn't me, is what I'm…

KENNETH. Then who was it? (*Pause*.) Who was it?

DOC. I don't know.

   Pause.

KENNETH. Because don't start saying it was me.

DOC. No.

KENNETH. Okay?

DOC. Yeah.

KENNETH. Okay.

   Pause.

   Do you not know I'm just pulling your peanut?

DOC. What?

KENNETH. I'm just pulling your peanut on you! I know it wasn't you!

DOC. Oh.

Pause. DOC *gives a little laugh*. KENNETH *smiles*.

KENNETH. You were probably nowhere near the place!

DOC. I know! I wasn't!

KENNETH. You've probably never been up there.

DOC. No!

KENNETH. Sure I'm only jockin' with ya! You like wrestling?

DOC. What?

KENNETH. The black eye.

DOC. Oh yeah... no it was...

KENNETH. It was an accident, was it?

DOC. Yeah.

KENNETH *finds* AIMEE*'s bag and starts looking through it*.

Are you... a friend of Tommy's?

KENNETH. Am I a friend of Tommy's?

DOC. Yeah.

KENNETH. Well, what would you call a friend?

Pause.

DOC. Someone who's friendly with him?

KENNETH. Mm-hm, what else?

DOC. What else?

KENNETH. Yeah, what else?

DOC. Well, like, do you know him?

KENNETH. Does anyone really know anyone? Though. You know what I mean? Like what would you call a friend?

DOC. Someone… you want to see?

Pause.

KENNETH. Did you see a girl in here?

DOC. A girl?

KENNETH. Yeah, a girl.

Long pause.

Is she here?

DOC. No.

KENNETH. Is she gone out with Tommy?

DOC. They're just gone down to check the Lotto.

KENNETH. Yeah, you told me that.

DOC. Oh yeah. (*Short pause.*) And maybe em…

KENNETH. Yeah?

DOC. Get some milk. I think.

KENNETH. And youse are in business?

DOC. Me and Tommy?

KENNETH. Yeah.

DOC. Yeah, I suppose.

KENNETH. So you're partners or…?

DOC. Yeah, partners, you know… Well, like Tommy owns the van. We might clear out somebody's shed or…

KENNETH. Okay.

DOC. Yeah. I don't drive but.

KENNETH. Okay.

DOC. Yeah. Keeping it real, you know.

Pause.

KENNETH. Okay. And are you in business with Aimee?

DOC. Oh no.

KENNETH. You're not.

DOC. No.

KENNETH. But Tommy is.

DOC. No... I don't think so. (*Pause*.) I think she's just staying here.

KENNETH. For work.

DOC. No I don't think so.

KENNETH. But, kind of... it's just really vague.

DOC. No, I don't... like... I'm...

KENNETH. Do you sleep in here?

Short pause.

DOC. Well, you know. Sometimes.

KENNETH. Where does Aimee sleep?

DOC. I think over there.

KENNETH. Where do you sleep? In there as well?

DOC. No, you see I just sleep here sometimes if we have an early start. I haven't slept here with Aimee here yet.

KENNETH. Not yet, no?

DOC. No.

Pause. KENNETH *regards* DOC.

KENNETH. Is your leg shaking?

DOC. I don't know.

KENNETH. Well, look I'll tell you: fear is not just one thing. There's that white-grey edge jagging in on your vision like a fucking car alarm? Or that black, kind of cold tiredness you get just from being worn out by being really scared for days on end, where you just want something bad to happen – just to [get it over with]...

DOC. Yeah.

KENNETH. Here, look at this.

> KENNETH *takes two rows of jagged fangs from his pocket and puts them in his mouth. He opens his mouth wide bearing the teeth, standing there looking at* DOC. *Pause.*

DOC. Yeah, that's... They're pretty eh...

> KENNETH *growls at* DOC. *Pause.*

(*Unsure.*) Ha ha ha...

> KENNETH *advances on* DOC, *growling.*

Ha ha ha.

> DOC *instinctively sits on* TOMMY's *bed.* KENNETH *approaches* DOC, *opens his arms over him, and roars down at him. Pause.*

Yeah... they're... pretty good.

> KENNETH *goes and gets the hammer. He stands over* DOC *again and roars down at him.* DOC *is now frozen in terror. Pause.* KENNETH *suddenly hits* DOC *with the hammer.*

Hey!

> KENNETH *hits him again.*

Hey! What the fuck are you doing?

> DOC *gets to his feet and backs away.* KENNETH *follows him. He swings the hammer at* DOC *again.*

Get off!

> KENNETH *follows him.*

Get off!

> KENNETH *follows* DOC *around the room.* DOC *tries to bolt for the door to the hallway but* KENNETH *blocks his way.* DOC *runs into the little toilet and tries to lock the door but* KENNETH *pushes his way in after him. We hear* DOC *crying out as* KENNETH *beats him. From above we hear*

MAURICE *banging down from upstairs in protest at the noise. After a few moments,* DOC *falls silent.* KENNETH *steps back into the room. There is blood on his suit and his face. He stands looking up at the ceiling. The thumping stops. The lights change, bringing us to late afternoon a few days later.* TOMMY *is alone, looking out into the garden while he listens to his phone. Long pause.*

TOMMY. What do you mean 'burnt'? Was the tinfoil itself burnt? (*Pause.*) Where was it? (*Pause.*) I don't know what people smoke off tinfoil, probably lots of things. Yeah! I know it's not good! Of course it's not good! (*Pause.*) What did you say to her? Well, why not? Maybe it's a school project for school or science or something. I don't know – an experiment! (*Pause.*) Well, how would I know? I left school when I was eleven! (*Pause.*) Of course I will – I'm happy to talk to her any time! That's…! Will she talk to me is the… I *am* gonna ring her! I told you I'd ring her! Yeah, I'll ring her, I won't text her. I'm run off my feet here, Suzanne, back up and down the bleeding hospital every day. Yeah. No he's… I don't know. Well, he's awake.

The door opens and MAURICE *stands there looking at* TOMMY. *There is a mean look about* MAURICE. *He has been drinking upstairs by himself for a few hours.*

(*Seeing* MAURICE.) Look I have to go. Yeah, I'll tell him. Yeah, I will, I'll call her tonight. I will! She knows I care! I do care! Jesus Christ…

He hangs up on her.

MAURICE. What haven't you put that woman through?

TOMMY. Oh… Don't you fucking start, Maurice.

TOMMY *looks for a bag.*

MAURICE (*drunkenly*). What?

TOMMY. Suzanne is no saint either, okay? (*Pause.*) So…

MAURICE (*amused*). Oh-ho!

TOMMY. Yeah, so… Before you…

MAURICE. Mm-hm…

TOMMY. You don't even know what you're talking about…

MAURICE. Look at the way you live.

During the following, TOMMY *starts stuffing some clothes into an old Liverpool FC sports bag.*

Look… at the way you live.

TOMMY. Look at the way you live…

MAURICE. I live alright, mate! At least I clean up after myself and I wash myself!

TOMMY. I wash myself, Maurice! For Jaysus' sake.

MAURICE. Look at the state of your clothes! What are you doing with them?

TOMMY. These are not my clothes! They're Doc's clothes.

MAURICE. Will you not iron them for him?

TOMMY. I don't have an iron.

MAURICE. I'll iron them, come on.

TOMMY. They'll do him. He's going to his sister's – let her bleeding do them.

MAURICE *watches* TOMMY *getting* DOC*'s clothes together.*

MAURICE. Can I ask you where you were earlier?

TOMMY. Where I always am! Back and forth up to the bleeding hospital, where do you think I was?

MAURICE. Did you forget?

TOMMY. Forget what?

MAURICE. Maura's anniversary mass. (*Short pause.*) At ten o'clock.

Pause.

TOMMY. Yeah. I forgot.

MAURICE. Yep.

TOMMY. Just with the... the circumstances.

Pause.

MAURICE. Yeah.

TOMMY. Oh just give me a break, Maurice, will you?

MAURICE. I said that girl was trouble. (*Short pause.*) Didn't I?

Pause.

Tommy.

TOMMY. What.

MAURICE. I said that girl was trouble, didn't I?

TOMMY. Yeah? Well, she's gone, so...

MAURICE. Yeah? Where?

TOMMY. I don't know.

MAURICE. What?

TOMMY. I don't know!

Pause.

MAURICE. You disgust me, Tommy.

TOMMY. I beg your pardon?

MAURICE. You disgust me.

TOMMY. I disgust you, do I?

MAURICE. I'm disappointed in you! I'm disappointed in you!

TOMMY. Maurice, at least I'm not drunk out of my mind at – what is it? Four o'clock in the afternoon!

Pause.

MAURICE. Do you know how many people were there? Do you know how many? Eight people, Tommy. Eight people for a whole life. Is that what it's all for? All the worry and all the battles? She wasn't talking to me, you see, so I didn't offer her my hand and anyway I was already down the road before I even realised it was icy and I just heard it – smack. And I turned around and there she was. Do you know what she said? She said, 'Maurice.' And I never felt so... And so... (*Gives a short shout of rage, and punches downward. Pause.*) Death is *real*, Tommy!

TOMMY. Oh for fuck's sake...

MAURICE. Yeah! You're just knocking the days off the calendar. There's even days when mass just takes you nowhere, just deposits you back on the pavement, just another invisible man, knowing that the end is sneaking in on you and knowing it's gonna be the worst part of your life. Looking at the news every night – for what? I don't even want to see it! What do I want to see some little girl with half her face hanging off in some bomb in some Arab country for? What can I do about it? And you feel like you have to witness all this fucking crap or else you're not a good person! What can I do about it?! And I look at you. You don't even know how lucky you are. You have two beautiful children and what do you do? You piss off on them! Fuck-arsing around with young ones...

TOMMY. Yeah well, it's not like that, Maurice.

MAURICE. What's it like then? Don't tell me what it's like! I know what it's like! Don't tell me what it's like, you little pup! I reared you, when no one else could cope with you. Maura had to toilet-train you! You were nearly four and a half!

TOMMY. Okay alright, Maurice.

TOMMY *struggles to close the zip on the bag.*

MAURICE. What?

TOMMY. Just go and lie down, will you?

MAURICE. And you bring whores in under my roof! Under my roof! A whore!

TOMMY *suddenly throws the bag across the room against the wall. It lands near the door.*

TOMMY. For fuck's sake, Maurice! Just fuck off, will you!?
Just fuck off!

Pause. TOMMY *sits disconsolately on the camp bed.*

MAURICE. Evil… has… no meaning. (*Pause.*) All I'm asking
– what happened to all that sweetness… is what I want to
know.

TOMMY. What sweetness?

MAURICE. When we used to go down the canal, and you
holding my hand, and asking me all the questions in the
world. And now the country is a shambles and we're crying
out for people like you. That can lead us into the light,
Tommy.

TOMMY. I'm just a moocher, Maurice.

TOMMY*'s mobile phone rings. He goes to answer it.*

That's all I ever was. Hello? (*Pause.*) Okay. It's alright, calm
down. Where are you? (*Pause.*) Well, just stay there. No, just
sit there. Take it easy! I'm coming! Okay?

TOMMY *hangs up and grabs his coat and his keys.*

MAURICE. Who's that?

TOMMY. Doc. His sister hasn't shown up to collect him and
they're kicking him out.

MAURICE. I'll come with you.

TOMMY. No, Maurice, come and lie down, will you?

TOMMY *tries to guide* MAURICE *out by the arm.*
MAURICE *pulls his arm away.*

MAURICE. No, I want to go and look at my vegetables.

TOMMY. Ah, suit yourself!

TOMMY *storms out with* DOC*'s clothes.* MAURICE *stands
there for a moment. He takes a small bottle of Irish whiskey
from his pocket and drinks from it. He goes to the double
doors and lets himself out to the balcony, going off down to*

*the garden. Time passes. A heavy dusk gathers in the room
and raindrops spatter the windows. After a few moments, the
door opens and* AIMEE *slips in quietly. She waits a moment,
listening, then goes to the loose floorboard and takes out the
biscuit tin with* TOMMY*'s money. She opens the tin and
starts counting money out on to the floor. When she has three
thousand euros she puts the rest back, replaces the lid, and
puts it back under the floorboard. As she goes to leave,*
KENNETH *appears in the doorway.*

AIMEE (*startled*). What are you doing!?

KENNETH. It's alright! There's nobody here!

AIMEE. Right, come on.

KENNETH. Woah, woah woah. How much did you get?

AIMEE (*showing him what she has taken*). Three thousand.

KENNETH. Don't mind that.

Pause.

AIMEE. You said three thousand.

KENNETH. Don't mind what I said.

AIMEE. There is no more, that's it.

Pause.

KENNETH. Alright you've made your point. You can leave that
there. (*Scatters money to the floor.*) Come on we'll get a
smoke.

AIMEE. No, I'm not doing that. Just take it.

She starts retrieving money from the floor.

KENNETH. Do you know what's so…? It's not even about any
of this. It's not about any of that.

AIMEE. Then what's it about?!

KENNETH. I'm on top of it.

AIMEE. What?

KENNETH. I'm on top of it. I got up on top of it and I...

AIMEE. What the fuck are you talking about?

KENNETH. I'm sorry! I'm sorry alright?

He tries to touch her. She recoils as though from an electric shock, pointing at him to stay away from her.

Those people wrote to you.

Pause.

AIMEE. What people?

KENNETH. The people. They wrote you a letter.

Pause.

AIMEE. Where is it?

Pause.

KENNETH. I read it for you.

Pause.

AIMEE. What did it say?

KENNETH. Ah, it was just... all this medical stuff.

AIMEE*'s face crumples.*

They'll keep you informed and all this but they're not gonna let you meet the little one. Because they think it'll only confuse her 'cause she's too young. (*Short pause.*) She's too young!

Pause.

AIMEE. Do you have it?

KENNETH. No.

AIMEE. Did it say what they call her?

He shakes his head.

KENNETH. Aimee, listen. She's better off and you're better off because unfortunately, you're not right in the fucking head. You're not right in the fucking head.

He gently strokes her arm.

Let's go, okay? Come on.

AIMEE *shakes her head.*

Aimee.

The menace in KENNETH*'s voice makes* AIMEE *look up at him. Pause. The door opens.* TOMMY *is standing watching them. Pause.*

Tommy! (*Comes to* TOMMY, *offering his hand.*) How are you?

TOMMY. What are you doing?

KENNETH. I'm not doing anything.

TOMMY. What are you doing with my money?

KENNETH. Tommy. We're bereaved.

Pause.

TOMMY. What do you mean?

KENNETH. Has Aimee not told you? (*Pause.*) Ah for Jaysus' sake! Her mother passed away a few weeks ago.

TOMMY. So?

KENNETH. Well, then this is a total misunderstanding! Listen, what's happened is we've had to move in with Aimee's mother in her house to look after her because she was in a virtual coma, or she might as well have been! (*Laughs.*) And then the doctor said that actually she was dead and her brother decided to break up the asset without any remuneration towards my… towards my… So Aimee has – if I am correct – decided to reimburse me, and because she's now within your… sphere going round your orbit she's dug in under your floor to borrow your resources to pay me back, with, I believe – Aimee? – the full intention of paying you back. So that's… who I am.

TOMMY. Yeah, I know who you are. Whatever your fucking name is.

KENNETH. That was self-defence, Tommy. She scratched me in the eye, for Christ's sake! (*Laughs.*) Aimee?

AIMEE *doesn't answer*.

Oh thanks! Listen, Tommy, I know how this looks. This looks fucking pathetic. That's fine then, we'll cut out the middle man. I'll call around here say every Saturday evening, Saturday night around eight o'clock, nine o'clock, we can keep it loose, or even every Sunday after dinner, you just give me an envelope, it's Aimee's instalments, that's fine, straight *i mo phóca*, I don't need a cup of tea, I've already eaten, I have somewhere I have to be, that's fine, see you next week. Ding dong. The week has flown by! That kind of thing.

TOMMY. Well no, I've a better idea. Why don't you just clear off out of here?

KENNETH. Me clear off?

TOMMY. Yeah.

KENNETH. Listen, there's no need to fly off the handle. (*Pause.*) You're saying to clear off and not come back?

TOMMY. Yeah.

KENNETH. Yeah come back or yeah not come back.

TOMMY. Not come back.

KENNETH. So just take this – (*Tin.*) and not come back.

TOMMY. No, leave that.

KENNETH. And not come back?

TOMMY. You're not taking that.

KENNETH. Well then I don't understand what's happening.

TOMMY. I don't give a fuck what you understand. Give me the box.

AIMEE. Tommy…

KENNETH. She says she's paying you back! (*To* AIMEE.)
    Right?

AIMEE. Tommy. I'm gonna pay you back.

KENNETH. In forty-euro instalments, right?

    Pause.

TOMMY. That's not the way it's gonna happen.

KENNETH. Well then will someone please explain to me what
    is gonna happen?

TOMMY. You give me the box and go. Both of you go.

    Pause.

    AIMEE *goes to leave.*

KENNETH. No wait, we're talking.

    She ignores him. He grabs her.

    We're talking!

    AIMEE *hits at his arm, trying to free herself.*

TOMMY. Hey now! Hey, hey, hey! Now, listen I don't give a
    fuck how youse go, together or separately or on your own or
    together, but you're not taking that box!

KENNETH. Well, you're not doing a lot to help the situation,
    are you?

TOMMY. What the fuck is your problem?!

KENNETH. *My* problem? Oh now *I* have a problem?!

TOMMY. Yeah, I'd say you have a problem! I'd say you have a
    lot of problems, yeah!

KENNETH. Oh yeah? (*Pushes* AIMEE *into the room towards*
    TOMMY, *building in agitation.*) Well, maybe my problem is
    it's like my eyes have been taken out and I just can't see
    what's in front of me like it's always night-time so when
    night-time really comes you think it feels like a relief except
    I can't sleep so that when it's morning it feels like it's

burning my brain and I drink too much coffee on my own
'cause you're going around everywhere with a clouded mind
trying to forget a devil lives inside you and you should
probably just go home but you can't do that so you're all the
time out and about and you're getting annoyed with people
because they won't listen and the same old same old is going
round and round and round and round and round and round
and round and round and round and round and round and
round and round and round until you start to fucking think
that maybe *that's* your problem!

Pause.

TOMMY. Look, you're not gonna take my money. I'll help
anyone out. Same as the next man, but I've got troubles. I've
got my own problems and you're not taking my money.

Pause.

KENNETH. You think you can love her?

TOMMY. What?

KENNETH. You think you can go up and down the courts with
her and talk to the solicitor about all her shoplifting charges?
And talk to the doctor about the time she managed to get
herself lost in town?

AIMEE. I'm not staying here for this!

AIMEE *starts to leave.*

KENNETH. We're still talking!

KENNETH *stops her and knocks her to the floor.*

TOMMY. Jesus Christ! What the fuck is wrong with you?

KENNETH. No, no, it's alright. It's alright. It's alright. Come
on. (*Kicks* TOMMY *on the bottom.*) Come on. It's alright!

AIMEE *grabs* KENNETH *from behind. He swings round
and throws her into the kitchen area with a clatter.*
KENNETH *turns to find* TOMMY *attacking him with the
biscuit tin. They wrestle and the tin falls to the ground.*

AIMEE *goes to the sink and grabs a bread knife. She grabs* KENNETH *from behind and sticks the knife into his back, leaving the handle protruding.* KENNETH *stops fighting and gets to his feet. He stands staring at* AIMEE. TOMMY *and* AIMEE *watch as* KENNETH *reaches up with his left hand to get at the knife but he cannot raise it high enough. He tries to raise his right hand but can only raise it a few inches. He tries to raise his left hand again but can hardly lift it at all. He walks towards* AIMEE. *She backs away. He halts and walks toward the window. He appears to be looking out at the fading light. He sits on the camp bed for a moment then lies down as though he is going to sleep. He lies completely still.* TOMMY *gets up and goes towards* KENNETH. *He stands over the body, staring at it for a moment before suddenly crying out in rage and striking it six or seven times while* AIMEE *watches him.* TOMMY *stands looking down at the body again. He is breathless and his hands are shaking. He puts his hand on* KENNETH's *throat and feels for a pulse. Dusk has darkened the room.* TOMMY *grabs a blanket and throws it over the body.*

AIMEE. What'll we do?

Pause.

TOMMY. We'll hide him.

AIMEE. Where? (*Pause.*) Where?

TOMMY. What do you mean 'where'? People disappear every day. People just go… (*Gestures.*) poff!

AIMEE *shakes her head.*

Yeah! And we can, we can… we can… we can just… We can just… go! Okay?

AIMEE. Go where?

TOMMY. Just go! Who cares? Finland.

AIMEE. Finland?

TOMMY. Finland is a beautiful country, Aimee. The light! You go off up into the forest. No one cares who you are.

Pause.

AIMEE. What about your kids?

TOMMY. They don't [need me]...! They're...

AIMEE raises her hand to her mouth. Her hand is shaking uncontrollably. TOMMY goes towards her. The door to the landing opens and MAURICE stands there, half-undressed, he wears stripy pyjama bottoms and a blazer over his vest. He seems even more inebriated.

MAURICE. What in the name of sweet fucking Jaysus is going on?

TOMMY. Nothing.

MAURICE. It doesn't fucking sound like nothing!

TOMMY. It's alright, Maurice. Go back to bed.

MAURICE. I'm not in bed!

TOMMY. We had a row, alright?

MAURICE (*sarcastically*). Oh yeah? (*To* AIMEE.) I knew the feather wouldn't blow too far – because there's too much shite on the egg! Hm? Hello to you too. Ha?

He suddenly starts singing a song, drunkenly serenading AIMEE. He looks over at the camp bed where KENNETH's body lies curled up.

What's that?

Silence. MAURICE walks over to the camp bed and peers down in the gloom. But rather than examine the body, he crouches and drags something out from under the bed. It is a sack of vegetables. He opens it and looks inside.

I fucking *knew* it! And you and that other gobdaw trying to tell me the crows had dug them up? The crows! What do you think I am? A nincompoop? Well, I have you now. Ha?

Explain that! (*Pause*.) You can't explain it. There is no explanation. A tiny modicum of respect, Tommy. That's all I've ever been talking about – that you might even ask me. (*Pause. To* AIMEE.) I don't even eat them! (*To* TOMMY.)You know that I can't! (*Takes the sack to the door, then turns*.) You know, Tommy? Maybe it's time you moved along, okay? I don't think this is working.

MAURICE *leaves*. TOMMY *and* AIMEE *stand there. Then* AIMEE *goes to the body and looks down at it.* TOMMY *watches her. She kneels beside the body. The lights go down and bring us to a bright morning two days later. The body is gone and* DOC *is sitting in the room. His head is bandaged. He has a dressing on his ear and two of his fingers are taped round a splint. He stares into space as though reliving what happened to him in here.* MAURICE *comes to the door wearing his dressing gown.*

Where's the other fella?

DOC. He's gone down the chemist. (*Pause*.) To get my prescription.

MAURICE. How are you doing?

DOC. What?

MAURICE. Are you on the mend?

DOC. Yeah, I have to go back on Monday they're gonna drain my ear again.

MAURICE. They're gonna what?

DOC. Drain it. Drain my ear.

MAURICE. Well, that doesn't sound so good.

DOC. Yeah? Well, they say it's to stop it becoming infected.

MAURICE. God. (*Pause*.) Well, that doesn't sound so good.

Pause.

DOC. So Tommy's moving out?

MAURICE. Mm.

DOC. The end of an era.

MAURICE. Hm.

DOC. Maurice, I want you to know, that it was me that dug up all your turnips. It wasn't Tommy. He told me not to be doing it.

Pause.

MAURICE. Tell Tommy I want to see him when he comes back, will you?

DOC. Yeah. I'm sorry, okay? If you want, I can call round and sort out the garden for you. I just didn't want to see it all going to waste.

MAURICE. Alright, well, I'm glad you're on the mend.

DOC. You should see the other fella.

MAURICE. Yeah?

DOC. Yeah, I milled him.

MAURICE. Yeah?

DOC. Yeah, I absolutely brainalised him.

MAURICE. Yeah?

DOC. Yeah.

MAURICE. Fair play to you.

MAURICE *goes.* DOC *adjusts his arm in his sling trying to get more comfortable. He is in considerable pain.* TOMMY *comes in the double doors from the balcony.*

DOC. You just missed Maurice, Tommy.

TOMMY *just nods, bringing a bag from the chemist to* DOC.

TOMMY. Here.

DOC. He was just in here looking for you.

TOMMY. Okay, here you go. (*A little box.*) This is an inhaler, you take that twice a day, morning and evening.

DOC. What is it?

TOMMY. You stick it up your nose and you press the button.

DOC. Oh yeah.

TOMMY (*taking out tablets*). If your headache gets really bad, you just take a half of one of these, alright? Otherwise just take two of these, they're paracetamol, and you take one of these – (*Another little box.*) every day. Alright?

DOC. Yeah, you can remind me.

TOMMY. Well, just, look it's all written there.

DOC. Yeah but just in case I forget.

TOMMY. But, Doc, I'm not gonna be here, man.

DOC. But where are you going?

TOMMY. No, I'm going away.

DOC. I thought you were just moving.

TOMMY. No I'm going away.

DOC. Away from Dublin?

TOMMY. I'm going abroad, man. I have a… I've an offer of work, so…

DOC. You need me to come with you?

TOMMY. No, I don't think I…

DOC. Where is it? Up in the north?

TOMMY. Yeah, up in the north. (*Pause.*) And maybe in Scotland as well, so you know…

DOC. And you're going now?

TOMMY. Yeah, I'm going now, I'm going this morning.

DOC. Now?

TOMMY. Yeah, now.

Pause.

DOC. What are you talking about?!

TOMMY. What do you mean what am I talking about? Didn't I just say it to you?

DOC. Well, I'll come with you if it's just Northern Ireland. I can mind the van.

TOMMY. No, it's gonna be abroad, Doc, so… you know.

DOC. Well, do you need me to mind the van?

TOMMY. I'm taking the van.

DOC. The van's gonna be gone?!

TOMMY. Yeah, the van is gonna be gone and I'm gonna be gone. Okay? Okay?

DOC. Oh.

TOMMY. Yeah so…

DOC. Yeah, no, that's… the only problem is…

TOMMY. What?

DOC. No, it's just, Teresa is saying I can't stay with her, so…

TOMMY. Well, what's that got to do with me?

DOC. No I was just…

TOMMY. What?

DOC. No I was just… I was hoping that… you wouldn't mind me staying here until my ear got better.

TOMMY. But I'm not gonna be here.

DOC. Yeah.

Pause.

TOMMY. I'm not gonna be here.

DOC. Yeah that's… That's the…

TOMMY. You're gonna have to do your own thing.

DOC. Yeah that's…

   TOMMY *is throwing his razor and toothbrush, etc., into a little bag.*

TOMMY. You know what I mean?

DOC. Yeah.

TOMMY. You'll have to get yourself sorted out.

DOC. I know.

TOMMY. I mean this is… you know… Maybe it's time you got serious anyway, you know?

DOC. Yeah.

TOMMY. Not fucking around and sleeping here and sleeping there. I mean, it's all a bit mad, Doc.

DOC. I know!

TOMMY. You know what I mean?

DOC. I know! It's mad.

TOMMY. It's… you know…

DOC. Listen, you don't have to tell me that. The only problem is I was hoping that I'd be able to… to just… be able to stay here.

TOMMY. You want to stay here. Talk to Maurice.

DOC. I don't have the rent.

TOMMY. You can get the rent! Go down the social welfare office.

DOC. Just talk to them in there…

TOMMY. Yeah, you go in, and you fucking… say… you know… I don't have any fucking money! Just tell them. The banks are bust, you need your rent, you know…

DOC. Yeah.

Pause.

TOMMY. Yeah? Okay?

DOC. Yeah, no that's…

Pause. DOC *exhales heavily.*

TOMMY. What?!

DOC. No, just, what am I gonna do?

TOMMY. What are you…? What have we just been talking about?

DOC. I know, but…

TOMMY. It's not up to me, Doc. (*Pause.*) Okay?

DOC. Yeah.

Pause.

TOMMY. Okay?

DOC. Yeah. (*Pause.*) No, it's just…

TOMMY. What.

DOC. Just you go in the hostels and… I'm just not able for all the fucking people in there, you know…

TOMMY. But you won't be in the hostels! Go down the social welfare. Go down now. Go down this morning.

DOC. Yeah but they say you're not on the books any more and you need a letter from your previous employer and then in the hostels you get all them, Batman, and Landline and all them fuckers, they take your runners, they take your shower gel…

TOMMY. But that's not [going to happen]…! Look, come here, look. (*Goes and takes some money from a coat pocket.*) Now, look, here we go, there's all your Christmas money. (*Pause.*) And this is… (*From his own pocket.*) Look, take this. That's from me. We'll call that a soft loan.

DOC. For how long?

TOMMY. For what how long?

DOC. For how long the loan…

TOMMY. I'm giving it to you, I'm giving it to you, okay? There you go. That's… now. Okay?

DOC stands there looking at the money in his hand while TOMMY goes and continues getting his stuff together.

DOC. Tommy?

TOMMY. Yeah?

Pause.

DOC. Did I tell you Maurice was looking for you?

TOMMY. Yeah you told me.

Pause.

DOC. Tommy…

TOMMY. Yeah? (*Pause.*) What?

Pause.

DOC. No, just em…

TOMMY. What? (*Pause.*) What? What's the matter with you? (*With sudden rage.*) Would you fucking leave me alone will you?! What's the matter with you? You're like a fucking stone brick around my neck every time I turn around you're coming in the fucking window! What's the matter with you?! Ha?

DOC. What?

TOMMY. What's the matter with you? What's wrong with you? (*Pause.*) What's wrong with you?!

Pause.

DOC. I don't know.

TOMMY. Ha?

DOC. I don't know.

Pause. AIMEE *comes in the door tentatively and stands there.*

I'll see you, Tommy.

DOC *leaves through the balcony doors and is gone.* TOMMY *stands and looks guiltily at* AIMEE. *Then he notices that* DOC *has forgotten his medications. He grabs the bag and goes to the balcony doors.*

TOMMY (*calls*). Doc! Doc! (*To himself.*) Fuck it.

He comes back into the room and throws the bag on the bed.

What are you doing? (*Pause.*) Where were you? I was looking for you all down the shops!

He goes and closes the door behind her.

AIMEE. I went for a walk.

TOMMY. A walk? Are you fucking mad?

AIMEE. You were asleep.

TOMMY. Well, I must have only fell asleep for a few minutes.

AIMEE. I couldn't wake you up.

TOMMY. Did you go and buy drugs?

AIMEE. No!

Pause.

TOMMY. I have it worked out. (*Shows her a piece of paper.*) We drive up to Belfast, get the ferry to Stranraer in Scotland, drive down through England to Harwich, ferry from Harwich to the Hook of Holland, drive up through Denmark to Frederikshavn – ferry to Gothenberg okay? In Sweden get to Kapellskär and ferry – bang – into Marienshaven. In Finland, we're there. It's that easy.

Pause.

AIMEE. That doesn't sound so easy though, Tommy.

TOMMY. Of course it's easy. Why isn't it easy?

AIMEE. Because I don't have a passport.

TOMMY. What? Why not?

AIMEE. I never had one.

TOMMY. Why didn't you tell me that?

AIMEE. I didn't think of it.

TOMMY. When did you not think of it, just now?

AIMEE. I don't know, this morning.

TOMMY. This morning? (*Angrily hissing his rage.*) You couldn't have not thought of that two nights ago and me breaking my bollocks digging a hole in the pitch dark down in the wilds of County fucking Wicklow, no?!

AIMEE. Just go without me.

TOMMY. What? (*Pause.*) Ah don't be ridiculous! Anyway, you don't need a passport for the ferry.

AIMEE. Why not?

TOMMY. I don't know. You just don't. Because you're in the European Union or something.

AIMEE. Tommy, that's an awful lot of ferries, someone is bound to want to check somewhere. (*Short pause.*) You should just go on your own.

TOMMY. I'm not gonna just go on my own, come on!

AIMEE. Why not?

TOMMY. What?

AIMEE. Why not?

TOMMY. Because! Because we're… Because we're…

AIMEE. Tommy, I did it. I did it.

TOMMY. What, do you think I'm gonna just leave you in the lurch? What kind of person do you [think I am]…?

AIMEE. But it's not your problem. Is it?

TOMMY. Oh right, maybe it was just your problem before, but now it's… It's too late for that now, isn't it?

Pause. AIMEE *shakes her head.*

AIMEE. I'll see you, okay?

TOMMY. But where are you gonna go? You don't have a passport! Where are you gonna go? Listen, I want to go to Finland!

AIMEE. Well, go to Finland. No one's stopping you!

TOMMY (*suddenly changing tack and becoming positive*). Look! We'll get you a passport! We'll get you one. We'll get it. I mean, why the panic?! How long does it take to get one? A few days?

AIMEE. It's not going to work, Tommy.

TOMMY. Why is it not gonna work?

AIMEE. It's just not going to work!

TOMMY. What's not gonna work?

AIMEE. Everything.

TOMMY. What are you talking about? Listen, fuck all that. We say how it works! We did what we had to do, and we'll… This is… This has… And maybe that's… (*Pause.*) I love you, Aimee, okay? I love you. Okay?

AIMEE. You don't even know me, Tommy.

TOMMY. I do know you. I do. I've always known you. I've always known you.

AIMEE. You're just lonely.

TOMMY. Lonely?! I'm not lonely!

AIMEE. You are. You're just lonely and no one has touched you in a long time. That's all it is.

TOMMY. No.

AIMEE. Tommy, I'm gonna go. Okay?

TOMMY. You think I'm just some... fool? Who doesn't know what's going on inside his own head? Like I don't fucking know what's going on? I know what's going on! I know, okay? I just feel like I always...

Pause. TOMMY *goes to her*.

Don't go.

Long pause. TOMMY *goes to his biscuit tin*.

AIMEE. Don't give me any money, Tommy.

TOMMY. No, take it.

AIMEE. No.

TOMMY. Why not?

AIMEE. Because there's no point.

Pause.

TOMMY. Don't do that. Please don't do that.

There is a knock. The door opens and MAURICE *is there in his grey slacks, black shoes, a white shirt, a tie and a blazer. Pause*.

MAURICE (*to* AIMEE). Are you still here?

AIMEE. No.

AIMEE goes to the door.

Bye, Tommy.

She goes. Pause.

MAURICE. Where's she going?

TOMMY. I don't know.

Pause.

MAURICE. Well, I wanted to em... May I have a word?

TOMMY. What?

MAURICE. May I have a word with you?

TOMMY. What do you want?

MAURICE. I have a… an appointment with my solicitor at four o'clock.

TOMMY. About the rent?

MAURICE. No, not about the rent. I eh… I don't want to end up in a… I… You see, I need to be able to live here right to the… (*Points at* TOMMY *with his open palm and makes a single clicking sound.*) So if you want to stay on, I'll… I'm going to leave you the house. And… (*Pause.*) okay?

No response.

Okay?

TOMMY *nods.*

Okay?

TOMMY (*quietly*). Yeah.

MAURICE. Well, don't get too fuckin' excited about it.

Long pause.

Is she coming back?

TOMMY *shakes his head.*

You're better off. You need a settled woman, Tommy. Someone who's settled in herself.

TOMMY. Yeah.

MAURICE. You only get a few goes, Tommy. At life. You don't get endless goes. Two three goes maybe. When you hit the right groove you'll click right in there. No drama. That's only for fucking eejits. (*Pause.*) This is it. (*Pause.*) Tommy.

Pause. The balcony doors rattle and DOC's *head appears.*

Oh here he is. The gay caballero.

DOC. There I am. I'm sorry. I forgot my prescription.

DOC *picks up the bag from the chemist.*

MAURICE. You forgot your what?

DOC. My prescription for the chemist.

MAURICE. Is it here?

TOMMY *brings it to* DOC.

DOC. Thanks, Tommy. Sorry I wouldn't have come back, only I knew you'd be gone so... Bye, Maurice.

TOMMY. Here, hang on. You're alright.

DOC. Nah, I won't stay.

TOMMY. You're alright.

Pause.

DOC. What, are you [two having a private conversation]...?

TOMMY. Come in.

DOC *stands inside the room. All three of them are silent.*

DOC. So, you're moving out later on or...?

TOMMY *shakes his head. Pause.*

MAURICE (*apropos of nothing*). Yeah.

Pause.

DOC. Does anyone... want a cup of coffee?

MAURICE. What kind of coffee?

DOC. Instant.

MAURICE (*as though this is preferable*). Oh instant? Yeah, I will.

DOC *goes to the sink to fill the kettle.* TOMMY *sits.* MAURICE *goes to the double doors and looks out at the garden.*

DOC. You see out there, the hedge and all that, Maurice?

MAURICE. Yeah.

DOC. I was thinking you should pull that all up.

MAURICE. Were you now?

DOC. Yeah, and look, where the sun is now? That's where you want to put down a patio where you go and sit in the morning.

MAURICE. Yeah?

DOC. Yeah, Tommy has paving blocks in the lock-up. Tommy?

TOMMY. Mm?

DOC. Paving slabs.

TOMMY. Yeah.

DOC. Me and Tommy dig it up, bang bang bang, a patio, a few chairs, put on your coat and your hat and your scarf, you sit out there in the evening, up the other end, and have your hot whiskey. Think about things.

MAURICE. Hm…

DOC. The sun going down behind the trees. Whistle up to Tommy. Hot whiskey please, Tommy!

MAURICE. Yeah, I'd be waiting a long time. I'd be freezing my balls off.

MAURICE *and* DOC *laugh, but they can't look* TOMMY *in the eye.*

DOC. Don't mind that. And look over all there. Dig all that out, turn it over, put down your few bulbs. Next thing you know, it's spring – and boom – all the flowers.

MAURICE. Yeah, I don't know. Maybe. (*Pause. Glances at* TOMMY.) Come down, show me what you mean.

DOC. Yeah, I'll show you. (*Off.*) Do you know what decking is, Maurice?

DOC *and* MAURICE, *uncomfortable with* TOMMY*'s withdrawn demeanour, walk down to the garden together while the lights change. A low afternoon sun creeps into the room catching* TOMMY *alone with his head in his hands.*

*Music takes us to a winter's evening. The music goes into the
radio and we find DOC alone in the room, fixing the plug on
some fairy lights. His bandages are gone. After a few
moments, TOMMY bustles in from the landing with his coat
on and a few bags from the shops.*

(*Without looking up.*) Aye aye.

TOMMY. What are you doing?

DOC. Fixing the Christmas lights.

TOMMY. It's only the bleeding tenth of November!

DOC. Yeah I know, but you know, get it done, it's not hanging
over you.

TOMMY. Did you clear up all them leaves out there?

DOC. Yeah I did that ages ago. I'm just waiting for the rest of
them to fall.

TOMMY (*giving up*). Right…

DOC. How did you get on?

TOMMY. Yeah, good.

DOC. How was Michelle?

TOMMY. Yeah good.

DOC. She talking to you?

TOMMY. Yeah. No, she was. (*Pause.*) She's having a baby.

DOC. A baby?!

TOMMY. Yeah. Suzanne is going bananas.

DOC. What's she gonna do?

TOMMY. Suzanne?

DOC. No, Michelle.

TOMMY. She's gonna start training to be a hairdresser.

DOC. Never be out of work.

TOMMY. I know.

DOC. Because even bald people get their hair cut.

TOMMY. I know.

DOC. The joke is on them because the sides and back still get all bushy.

TOMMY. Yeah, but I'd say the idea of cutting auld baldy lads' hair is not where she's at.

DOC. No but I mean, if you had to. You can always earn a few bob.

TOMMY. Well, yeah.

DOC. Just watch, she'll be in here cutting all our hair for us. Grandkids will be running all over the house and she'll be trimming all the hair in your ears and your nose and everything.

TOMMY. I doubt it somehow.

DOC (*convinced he is right*). I don't know. (*Pause.*) There's beans in that pot on the ring.

TOMMY. Is there no sausages left?

DOC. Eh, no.

TOMMY. Just as well I got some. Do you want one?

DOC. Yeah I'll have a few more.

Pause.

TOMMY. Listen, I wasn't gonna go but… She's invited us to her eighteenth.

DOC. Tonight?

TOMMY. Yeah.

DOC. You and me?

TOMMY. Yeah, you and me and Maurice.

DOC. Will we go?

TOMMY. Do you want to go?

DOC. Will Suzanne mind us being there?

TOMMY. It's not up to her.

> DOC *concentrates on the lights. Pause.*

DOC. Maurice is gone down to The Little Nibble to have his dinner.

TOMMY. Do you think he'd want to?

DOC. I'd say he would.

TOMMY. Alright, well… I'll get changed.

> DOC *plugs in the lights. They come on.*

DOC. Here listen, thanks for the runners.

TOMMY. Oh yeah, are they alright?

DOC. Perfect, check it out. (*Comes and stands quite close to* TOMMY.) They give me another half an inch.

TOMMY. Oh yeah.

> TOMMY *takes some shirts from a bag from the dry cleaner's and starts taking one out of the plastic wrapping.* DOC *goes for his jacket.*

DOC. Oh here, em, Mick Mounfield was in the bookies' earlier with those twins, Romulus and…

TOMMY. Remus?

DOC. No Romulus and…

TOMMY. Remus?

DOC. No! What do you keep saying 'Remus' for? Is that even a name? No, what do you call them, the Casey twins, Romulus and… Dwayne Casey.

TOMMY (*does not know them*). Okay…

DOC. Mick Mounfield was in there with them and he told me that he saw… he said he saw… em…

> *Short pause.*

TOMMY. Aimee?

DOC. Yeah, but I don't think he's right. I didn't think he described her right.

TOMMY. Where was she?

DOC. He said he saw her sitting on the steps at the Custom's House but he said he thought she was about fifty years old. So it couldn't...

TOMMY. No.

DOC....couldn't have been her. But, you know, I always keep an ear out.

TOMMY. Yeah.

DOC. 'Cause my hunch is that she's alright.

TOMMY. Yeah?

DOC. Yeah.

TOMMY. Yeah.

Pause.

DOC. Will I tell you the good thing about Christmas? No one can turn you away. You see that light in the window. In you go.

TOMMY. Yeah. But you can't save everybody though, can you? I mean...

DOC. Yeah, I suppose. (*Pause.*) Here, do you know what a black hole is?

TOMMY. A black what?

DOC. A black hole.

TOMMY. In space?

DOC. Yeah. Do you know what it is?

TOMMY. Eh yeah, it's a... What is it?

Pause. DOC *has his jacket on. He is near the door.* TOMMY *is sorting out his clothes.* DOC *is lost in thought for a moment.*

DOC. No, I had a mad dream. Before I woke up. (*Pause*.) I had to write it down.

He goes to the camp bed and takes a piece of notepaper up.

TOMMY. Are you alright?

DOC. Yeah, no, it was just... I woke up and there was an old chap sitting there and do you know who he was?

TOMMY. Who?

DOC. He was one of the three wise men.

TOMMY. What he told you that or...?

DOC. No, you know the way you just know.

TOMMY. Okay.

DOC. And he was looking out the doors there up into the sky. And I sat up in the camp bed and he saw me and he said that when a star... dies, okay? It collapses into itself and its gravity is an unbelievable force, right? Not even light is quick enough to escape. He said that's why it's called a black hole. And he said that the faster you travel, the slower time goes, okay? And he said that if you ever came near a black hole you'd be sucked in so fast – faster and faster and faster – that time would slow down so slowly and it would take you so long to reach the heart of the dying star that you would never actually arrive, because at that speed, time, itself, becomes meaningless. So a black hole is a place, he said, where there is... no time. And he said that all the stars in our galaxy, and all... our sun, and all... everything is just spinning round and round a black hole. And he said that when you consider this fact: that we are all just going round a place where there is no time, how can any man say there is no God?

Pause.

I had to write it down.

TOMMY. Yeah, well, that's a heavy fucking dream right there man.

DOC. Yeah. (*Pause.*) Well, I'll go and get Maurice.

TOMMY. Yeah.

DOC. I'll see you in about fifteen, twenty minutes.

TOMMY. Yeah. In fifteen or twenty measurements of time.

They smile.

DOC. Yeah in fifteen or twenty units of time. I mean, like, time… What is it? You know what I mean?

TOMMY. Yeah, I know. Maybe you'll go down to The Little Nibble and never come back!

DOC. I know!

TOMMY. Doc, use the front door.

DOC goes to the main door.

DOC (*at the door*). Oh and he told me to tell you what Heaven is, Tommy.

TOMMY. Oh yeah?

DOC. Yeah, apparently, when you die, you won't even know you're dead! It'll just feel like everything has suddenly… come right, in your life. Like everything has just clicked into place and off you go.

TOMMY. Oh well, that's good, isn't it?

DOC. Yeah!

DOC leaves and TOMMY starts to get ready. He turns up the radio. A plaintive song is playing. He quickly washes his face in the sink. He puts on his clean shirt and goes into the little toilet.

For a few moments the room is empty except for the music. Then the balcony doors open and AIMEE silently steps into the room. She looks in good shape. She wears a new leather jacket, jeans and boots. She carries a bag with a strap which she puts down on the floor. She stands there while TOMMY comes back into the room. He does not see her at first. He goes to the mirror and combs his hair. After a few moments he sees AIMEE's *reflection and turns.*

They stand looking at each other. For a moment he wonders if she is real. Darkness falls.

www.nickhernbooks.co.uk

facebook.com/nickhernbooks

twitter.com/nickhernbooks